Victorian Culture in America, 1865–1914

PRIMARY SOURCES
IN AMERICAN HISTORY

Editor
Professor Grady McWhiney

IMPERIALISTS VERSUS ANTI-IMPERIALISTS:
The Debate Over Expansionism in the 1890's

Edited by **Richard E. Welch, Jr.**

OVER THERE: EUROPEAN REACTION TO
AMERICANS IN WORLD WAR I

Edited by **Robert C. Walton**

SLAVERY IN AMERICA: Theodore Weld's
American Slavery As It Is

Edited by **Richard O. Curry** and
Joanna Dunlap Cowden

AMERICAN UTOPIANISM

Edited by **Robert S. Fogarty**

CHILD-REARING CONCEPTS, 1628-1861
A Book of Sources
Philip J. Greven, Jr.

VICTORIAN CULTURE IN AMERICA
1865-1914

H. Wayne Morgan

VICTORIAN CULTURE IN AMERICA 1865-1914

H. WAYNE MORGAN
Professor of History
UNIVERSITY OF OKLAHOMA

F. E. PEACOCK PUBLISHERS, INC.
ITASCA, ILLINOIS 60143

JOHN W. CAUGHEY, Advisory Editor

For Anne

Foreword

It is not easy to understand the past. A good textbook helps by providing what its author—usually a distinguished historian—considers the essential facts and his interpretation of those facts. A good instructor also helps. But the student, if he is to be other than a parrot, must be exposed to more than one or two viewpoints. Told that authorities disagree, the student is likely to ask: "But which interpretation is *right?*"

At that point he is ready to do some research himself—to read and to evaluate what certain persons who actually saw an event wrote about it. Sampling original sources on which historical interpretations are based is not only an exciting experience; it adds flavor to knowledge. Furthermore, it encourages the student to weigh conflicting evidence himself and to understand historical variety and complexity.

The Primary Sources in American History series provides the documents necessary to explore the past through the eyes of those who lived it. Edited and introduced by an able scholar, each volume in the series contains contemporary material on some historical topic or period—either a collection of varied sources (letters, diaries, memoirs, reports, etc.), or a new edition of a classic eyewitness account.

Grady McWhiney
Editor

Table of Contents

Introduction

It is a truism that the United States "came of age," and "entered into world affairs" in the late 19th century. This process was most dramatic in economics and diplomacy, but America's cultural involvement with the world was equally striking. The industrial growth that produced a great economy also made many Americans aware of and eager to acquire cultural status. The leaders of brawling and dynamic cities endowed museums, symphony orchestras, opera houses, and libraries. They planned cities, and collected paintings and statuary. The nation was eager to show concern for more than money-making.

Improved communications and travel facilities allowed an increasing number of Americans to satisfy their curiosity about older civilizations. Students, especially of the arts, traveled in Europe, both to gain formal training and to sample the legacies of the past. Those unable to travel could read analyses of the arts in a rich new supply of periodicals, newspapers, and books.

Four major themes marked America's cultural development, as they marked its growth and change in other sectors. The art-public was open to innovative ideas and experimentation. Art became a means of improving or elevating the individual, and at the same time of promoting social stability in a turbulent period. Americans also desired to prove that the New World could produce a culture comparable to that of the Old; one that matched progress in government and economics. And like other peoples conscious of national development, Americans tried to retain a distinctive native quality in their arts within a world culture.

The sudden influx of ideas, increased wealth, and the need for durable artistic forms all inevitably produced confusion. But growth and change in the arts gave Americans a fresh sense of power and appreciation. Culture was as significant as diplomacy and economics in marking the interdependence of the Old World and the New.

I

Materialism and Culture

The average American traveler of the late 19th century probably felt inferior standing before the "Mona Lisa," or in Westminster Abbey. Americans praised the new, which they represented, yet naturally desired the reassurances of an orderly past. Mark Twain's *Innocents Abroad* (1869) well stated the American's alternating disdain for the "old world," and his subterranean fear that the new Republic was culturally inferior. Would America develop an exemplary culture to equal its political democracy and material power?

More and more Americans set out to prove their country's cultural merits, and were sensitive to the frequent charge of being materialistic. Envy doubtless motivated many such criticisms, and Americans simply had more resources to exploit than did European counterparts. But they also had different attitudes, oriented toward experiment and individual consumption. Other peoples hoarded wealth, revealing pessimism and a fear of poverty; Americans used it, testifying to a sense of abundance and optimism. Americans also prized mobility, choice, and convenience more than mere possessions. Money expanded personal freedom by increasing choices; the problem was how to combine utility and enduring taste. Foreign visitors noted that in no other country did wealthy men so readily support civic improvements. Nowhere else were so many cultural facilities available to the public.

The American utilitarian tradition required that everything "pay its way" with practical results, an attitude that had long penalized the arts. But in a time of sudden change and uncertain directions, culture became a stabilizing influence to many men. Art would "pay its way" by making its owner or beholder more sensitive to "higher" things, more civilized, and therefore more responsible to society. Desire for home decoration, and patronage of artists were sure signs to many observers of social and individual progress.

A desire for the "finer things" of life accompanied America's economic growth. What is good? and What is suitable? were the great cultural questions.

1. THE STRUGGLE FOR WEALTH

No one can settle down in a European city or village for a month, and observe the laboring classes, without noticing a great difference between their aspirations, ambitions and habits, and those of corresponding classes in this country. He may see great poverty in a continental town, and men and women laboring severely and faring meanly, and a hopeless gap existing between classes; he may see the poor virtually the slaves of the rich; but he will witness a measure of contentment and a daily participation in humble pleasures to which his eyes have been

Scribner's Monthly [*Century Magazine*], 8 (August, 1874), 495–96.

strangers at home. There is a sad side to this pleasant picture. Much of this apparent contentment and enjoyment undoubtedly come from the hopelessness of the struggle for anything better. An impassable gulf exists between them and the educated and aristocratic classes—a gulf which they have recognized from their birth; and, having recognized this, they have recognized their own limitations, and adapted themselves to them. Seeing just what they can do and cannot do, they very rationally undertake to get out of life just what their condition renders attainable. There is no far-off, crowning good for them to aim at, so they try to get what they can on the way. They make much of fête-days, and social gatherings, and music, and do what they can to sweeten their daily toil, which they know must be continued while the power to labor lasts.

In America it is very different. A humble backwoodsman sits in the presidential chair, or did sit there but recently; a tailor takes the highest honors of the nation; a canal-driver becomes a powerful millionaire; a humble clerk grows into a merchant prince, absorbing the labor and supplying the wants of tens of thousands. In city, state and national politics, hundreds and thousands may be counted of those who, by enterprise, and self-culture, and self-assertion, have raised themselves from the humblest positions to influence and place. There is no impassable gulf between the low and the high. Every man holds the ballot, and, therefore, every man is a person of political power and importance. The ways of business enterprise are many, and the rewards of success are munificent. Not a year, nor, indeed, a month, passes by, that does not illustrate the comparative ease with which poor men win wealth or acquire power.

The consequence is that all but the wholly brutal are after some great good that lies beyond their years of toil. The European expects always to be a tenant; the American intends before he dies to own the house he lives in. If city prices forbid this, he goes to the suburbs for his home. The European knows that life and labor are cheap, and that he cannot hope to win by them the wealth which will realize for him the dream of future ease; the American finds his labor dear, and its rewards comparatively bountiful, so that his dream of wealth is a rational one. He, therefore, denies himself, works early and late, and bends his energies, and directs those of his family into profitable channels, all for the great good that beckons him on from the far-off, golden future.

The typical American never lives in the present. If he indulges in a recreation, it is purely for health's sake, and at long intervals, or in great emergencies. He does not waste money on pleasure, and does not approve of those who do so. He lives in a constant fever of hope and expectation, or grows sour with hope deferred or blank disappointment. Out of it all grows the worship of wealth and that demoralization which results in unscrupulousness concerning the methods of its acquirement. So America presents the anomaly of a laboring class with unprecedented prosperity and privileges, and unexampled discontent and discomfort.

There is surely something better than this. There is something better than a life-long sacrifice of content and enjoyment for a possible wealth, which, however, may never be acquired, and which has not the power, when won, to yield its holder the boon which he expects it to purchase. To withhold from the frugal wife the gown she desires, to deny her the journey which would do so much to break up the monotony of her home-life, to rear children in mean ways, to shut away from the family life a thousand social pleasures, to relinquish all amusements that have a cost attached to them, for wealth which may or may not come when the family life is broken up forever—surely this is neither sound enterprise nor wise economy. We would not have the American laborer, farmer and mechanic become improvident, but we would very much like to see them happier than they are, by resort to the daily social enjoyments which are always ready to their hand. Nature is strong in the young, and they will have society and play of some sort. It should remain strong in the old, and does remain strong in them, until it is expelled by the absorbing and subordinating passion for gain. Something of the Old World fondness for play, and daily or weekly indulgence in it, should become habitual among our workers. Toil would be sweeter if there were a reward at the end of it; work would be gentler when used as a means for securing a pleasure which stands closer than an old age of ease; character would be softer and richer and more childlike, when acquired among genial, everyday delights. The all-subordinating strife for wealth, carried on with fearful struggles and constant self-denials, makes us petty, irritable and hard. When the whole American people have learned that a dollar's worth of pure pleasure is worth more than a dollar's worth of anything else under the sun; that working is not living, but only the means by which we win a living; that money is good for nothing except for what it brings of comfort and culture; and that we live not in the future, but the present, they will be a happy people—happier and better than they have been. "The morrow shall take thought for the things of itself," may not be an accepted maxim in political economy, but it was uttered by the wisest being that ever lived in the world, whose mission it was to make men both good and happy.

2. THE FIELD OF ART

Small straws show which way the wind blows. And nothing more truly indicates a people's advancement in matters of artistic judgment than its attitude toward the little things of life, the details of its surroundings. The average citizen is timid of asserting his "inalienable right" to a vote in disposing of the larger public art-commissions. Accordingly, by giving its works of this sort into the hands of men of large reputation, and by entrusting them with complete liberty in design, a community sometimes gets a substantial bit of good art in spite of itself. But this same average citizen is "bumptious" enough in tyrannizing over

Scribner's Magazine, 20 (September, 1896), 389–90.

the architect and the furnishers of his own home, and the result has been that, in this Nation of Homes, the artist, to whom bad taste in furnishings is the most discomforting of all inhospitalities has been a social outcast from almost the whole country.

The evolution of artistic judgment in a people passes, more or less gradually, through these stages: First, there is a scramble for the bare necessaries of life; herein, of course, artistic matters must go by the board in practical entirety. Then follows the lust of gain; and finance is the chief art practised. At length comes the realization that the community is rich. With this rises the passion for ostentation. The wealth of the community is advertised more or less blatantly, and artists are summoned primarily to display the opulence of their client. After the barrenness of the first estate, the sordid neglect even of comfort in the second, and the noisy splendor of the third, comes a generation born into commercial stability and into a leisure that opens the eye to refinement, to culture and to the ugliness of the paternal gew-gaws. This generation seeks its graces in a large simplicity and a perfect fitness of each thing for its function. It recognizes the eternal compromise between utility and beauty.

The salutary decrease in bric-a-brac is a case in point. The usual drawing-room grew, from a funereal and awesome mystery opened only on state occasions, to an inextricable mass of curios, heaped up without rhyme or reason on cabinets, whatnots, tables, door-frames, mantles, brackets—everywhere; until the general appearance of the place resembled a junk-shop more than a reception-room for friends, and the slightest movement was actually dangerous. The eye found no satisfaction, the body no comfort; and even the bric-a-brac was at a disadvantage from its very superabundance. But now, unfortunately for the curio-dealer, though happily for the nerves of the artistic, a soberer sense is bringing order out of the wreck, and the beauty of free space, the charm of unencumbered roominess, and the elegance of a rich simplicity, assert themselves increasingly in American homes.

Office and club-house furniture is showing the same wholesome spirit. Where desk-chairs, lounging-chairs, and divans were once as ornate, as stiff, and as hard as a Gothic cathedral—and about as comfortable to sit on—one now finds a tendency to substitute great arrangements in buxom leather, inviting and soothing. Even the street-cars and ferry-boats show the evolution. Formerly they were upholstered in garish stuffs and elaborated with complex friezes and gaudy panels. Many an artist, struggling then for his very life, though now grown into prosperity—one might mention even a recently elected Associate of the Royal Academy—many an artist of present fame executed these artistic burdens that cumbered the old boats and street-cars and the old Broadway stagecoaches.

The ferries and street-cars are now built more sensibly of light woods, managed with great simplicity, yet with eminently satisfactory effect. Indeed, there are many pretentious works of art—or, at art—that have less grace and taste than the Broadway cablecars with their plain light woods, their undecorated interiors, their simple lettering and their severe outlines conformed primarily to directness and utility. Our sleeping-cars, unfortunately, have hardly yet emerged from the stratum of knick-knackery and gloom, though, to relieve the tedium of travel, they have especial reason to display good taste.

The large hotels of the larger cities are a tremendous power for evil, where they might be missionaries for all that is good in art. The *nouveaux-riches* from the smaller cities, and the well-to-do of the larger towns, coming to the metropolis, put up at the widest-famed hostelries and accept as the gospel of best taste—"art," they call it—whatever manifestations of apocryphal judgment they see there. A massive pile of architectural gingerbread is the exterior to an interior of equally meaningless frippery. Gaudy ceilings, beds and chairs groaning with embellishments, dining-rooms of riotous design, offices of divers marbles and over-much gilt, parlors of oppressive elegance—these are set up at once as the ideals of beauty, the summit of good art. When the pilgrim goes back home he carries perverted standards that will prove a huge impediment to the judgment of many a later generation.

Still, the new movement for better standards is in the air, and a better day is on the horizon of American art-life. Its full coming will be marked by a general appreciation of the value of simplicity, breadth, and honest utility.

3. ART IN THE HOME

Most men get their chief education in the school of life and not in academic halls, and even those to whom fortune opens the doors of the university seldom take home with them the knowledge of any other art than the art poetic. The arts of drawing and music, it is true, have at last begun to receive some attention in our public schools, and this is well. Instruction in the art of design is also easily obtainable in most of our large cities. The fact, nevertheless, remains essentially as stated—that what most people know about art they have learned without instruction, simply by using their own eyes. Skill in art they have none; knowledge of the principles of art, little or none; appreciation of art, more or less, according to the degree in which they have been favored by circumstances.

It follows that the home must necessarily be the chief nursery of art for all but a favored few. But how and to what extent is home education in art possible? Certainly very little can be done in the way of technical training apart from competent instruction; but that which is of much more importance than any formal schooling can be acquired by most, namely, some appreciation of and consequent delight in whatever appeals to the cultivated esthetic sense. In point of fact, even now, in our own country, that home is the rare exception in which no picture hangs upon the walls, to bear witness to at least the blind groping after that which shall satisfy nature's longing to see either her real or her ideal self painted upon the netted curtain of the human eye.

The influence of dwelling habitually in the presence of a striking work of art can hardly be overestimated, whether the work be of such a character as to debase or to ennoble. The pencil of the artist is bribed to make the den of vice doubly alluring to the intoxicated senses of the reveler, while the glowing ardor of the religious devotee rises almost to ecstasy as he

The Chautauquan, 8 (October, 1887), 54–55.

gazes long upon some vivid representation of the tragedy of Calvary. As are the pictures upon the walls of the home, so are the pictures hung invisible to all but ourselves in the chambers of the imagination, where, night and day, they make much of the real world in which we live. Whether we dwell day by day with a picture or with a human being, the influence of the companionship is hardly greater in the latter case than in the former. Who has not, at some time in his life, been forcibly impressed by the circumstance, utterly meaningless in itself, of his eyes seeming to meet the gaze of a portrait hanging upon the wall? Beneath the subtle influence thus streaming from a lifeless canvas, many a beholder, no doubt, has been swayed as by a supernal power, and felt himself urged on or held back in some debated course.

It is not every work of art which has an ethical value; but the picture or the statue which simply charms the eye and goes no further may yet fulfill a worthy mission,—for the simple enjoyment of beauty is as legitimate an affection of the mind as any other. So that the sentiment of the work be pure, we need not demand of it a moral lesson.

One good work of art does more to beautify the home than a crowd of inferior productions. It is better to save our pennies for years, until with the accumulation something really good can be purchased, than to fritter away our resources upon what will give no lasting pleasure. Let us, if possible, have pictures which, from their excellence, there is no chance of our outgrowing. This is far from impossible, even to those whose circumstances necessitate strict economy, now that the sun has taken to being an artist and furnishes to all comers excellent fac-similes of the best that the skill of man has ever been able to produce. The camera, the graver's tool, and the printing-press have brought to every man's door almost every treasure of art.

II

New Influences

American artists worked abroad in the early 19th century, but the post-Civil War era saw an exodus of young talents to Europe. They studied in Paris with famous academicians, and reveled in the city's artistic atmosphere. Many went to Italy and Germany, and a few to England. There were major colonies of expatriate American artists in London and Paris. James A. McNeill Whistler lived in London, and John Singer Sargent was a thoroughgoing expatriate and world renowned celebrity. American artists exhibited the same curiosity and eagerness to learn that characterized traveling engineers, scientists, or teachers. Their enthusiasm was partly responsible for increasing interest in the old masters of several countries, and they were a major factor in reviving museum-going as a form of education by sight. The men and women trained abroad fertilized American art-thinking, criticism and teaching upon returning home. Above all, they developed a sharp sense of their roles as artists, with considerable impact on the art-public.

Several specific new influences shaped both American and world art. Oriental tastes and products had influenced earlier Americans, but became a major aspect of postwar art. Whistler popularized many Japanese attitudes and techniques, and Eastern influences affected the work of many important painters in both Europe and the United States. The following article is a good summary of what American critics saw in the methods and aims of Oriental art. It also reveals indirectly what they presumed about Western painting, and marks a growing interest in the abstract and nonrealistic in painting.

France played a special role in American art history; its masters produced many pupils, and there was an American market for their Academic pictures. But American critics and painters found Impressionism more durable and interesting than products of the Academies. Impressionism posed several critical problems to Americans. A people always interested in realistic portrayal of nature at first found the Impressionists' concern for the fleeting qualities of life puzzling. The Impressionists' frank delight in sensuous color and "painterly" qualities clashed with American earnestness in judging the moral merits and purposes of painting. But Americans were moving rapidly toward appreciating the subjective qualities in art. The Impressionists' depiction of routine daily living, which shocked European critics concerned with retaining painting's formalistic qualities, did not disturb Americans. And the Impressionists' landscape painting suited American taste, despite differences of opinion over the qualities of nature that painters should depict.

American critics were cautious in accepting advanced Impressionists. Monet became the standard of measurement for those still concerned to retain a sense of formal development in Impressionist painting. But the American art-public rather quickly accepted the style. The Paris dealer Durand-Ruel exhibited Impressionist works in an American tour in 1886. American painters accepted and experimented with the style. Sargent, the expatriate Mary Cassatt, and several American Impressionist painters such as J. Alden Weir, helped secure major Impressionist works for American museums and collectors. By the 1890s, Impressionism had triumphed in American art circles, and soon provided the grounds for yet another cyclical revolt against an academic formula.

Photography also affected artistic development. It revealed the limits of traditional realism, and emphasized the importance of the artist's interpretive abilities.

4. SOME ASPECTS OF JAPANESE PAINTING

WALTER M. CABOT

. . . The Japanese mind shows itself here, as elsewhere, to belong, generally speaking, to that class whose attitude toward art we term formal or classic. Japanese painting, indeed, had its periods of comparatively romantic and individualistic inspiration. Yet when regarded as a whole, and judged from our modern point of view, it will be seen to be essentially classic in spirit.

Firstly, the primary aim of the Japanese, as of every classic artist, is to reveal the various kinds of beauty which the nature of his art places at his command. The Oriental, for instance, sees in his lines and colors, his darks and lights, the means whereby he can create a sort of visual symphony, which, like the musical, shall produce its effect to a large extent independently of external aid. In other words, ideas that are attached to the elements of his art merely by chance association—ideas, that is to say, which are not essentially plastic—do not play a vital part in his aesthetic intention. But this is the classic viewpoint in a nutshell. For the most characteristic feature of classic art is the fact that the visible image and the thoughts it suggests are indissolubly fused.

Again, the Japanese painter takes special pleasure in certain other qualities which distinguish classic art,—lucidity, order, and finish; and his work gives us that sense of harmony and poise which constitutes plastic beauty.

The luxuriant symbolism which is often found in Japanese art does not, to my mind, disprove its classic intention. Symbolic form is in itself no evidence of a lack of classic taste. It is employed in Greek art. Only when it serves to express ideas the meaning of which cannot be conveyed otherwise is it an indication of subjective mystical feeling, of an unclassic frame of mind. Now the use of symbolism in the religious art of Japan, as in that of Greece, is to a large extent traditional. When

Atlantic Monthly, 95 (June, 1905), 804–13.

Buddhism was introduced from China in the sixth century A.D., symbolism already formed an integral part of it. Buddhistic symbolism is, however, essentially mystical; and it may be urged that the fact of its having preserved in Japan this quality in undiminished vigor proves that it touched a sympathetic chord in the Japanese nature. This, I believe, is true. There is undoubtedly a tinge of mysticism in the Japanese, as in all Orientals. But it remains largely a detached and independent factor in their mental life. For a study of the mind of this Eastern people will show that, while on the one hand it is dreamy and poetic, on the other it is extremely clear, objective, sane. That it is this lucidity of mind which primarily controls their art appears to me indisputable. Most of the arts of Japan have a superadded symbolic meaning: for example, flower arrangement, landscape gardening, poetry, and the dance; yet in respect to formal beauty they are complete in themselves. The understanding of this symbolism is not necessary to an appreciation of their essential charm. The Japanese garden is a complete work of art, even though one may not realize that these stones and trees are symbolically related; their floral designs delight the eye without the observer recognizing the emblem of filial love or wifely devotion. Even when, as in painting, the symbol becomes obvious, assumes definite shape, the work tells as an artistic whole, though the significance of the emblem be unknown. Forever sensitive to what is decoratively effective, they beautify it in such a way as to make it harmonize with and enrich the total effect. In the eyes of the Japanese public the symbolism of their art undoubtedly forms a special element of beauty; but to the Japanese painter its chief value lies in its decorative possibilities. For the ideas which are of primary interest to him, and which he strives to express on paper, are such as cannot be detached from their pictorial setting.

In a word, we find in the paintings of the Japanese—and this is a quality which makes them greater artists than poets— that classic delicacy of fancy characteristic of a Greek bas-relief, or a landscape by Corot; but there is wanting every indication of that imagination which, in its romantic tendencies, shuns all definition, and refuses to be guided by rule.

The student of Japanese painting is likely to be impressed first of all by its inventive fecundity. The fertility of the Oriental mind in devising fresh and ever delightful pictorial schemes for treating even the simplest subject has, I believe, never been surpassed. I examined one day some three hundred designs in stencil collected at random in a shop in Paris, and while each that I took up seemed more beautiful than the last in its decorative arrangement, I failed to note any duplication of design. This richness of invention is seen in all forms of Japanese art.

Another striking quality of Japanese, as of all the best classic art is the perfection which it attains within its self-imposed limits. This perfection is due, not merely to the technical ability of the Oriental artist, which makes it possible for him to give us the peculiar pleasure which we always take in the thing most directly and perfectly expressed, but also to a very pure and delicate aesthetic feeling. The way, for instance, in which line and color, light and dark, are made to echo, and thus intensify, the dominant emotional note of a picture, illustrates the sensitiveness of this Eastern people to the most subtle aesthetic effects.

The ability to discover beauty in the simplest thing, and to express it in such a way that the emotional effect to be conveyed reaches the beholder free from any irrelevant or disturbing element, gives to Japanese pictorial treatment largeness and dignity,—a certain "savor of the universal."

Perhaps the most remarkable quality of Japanese painting, however, is its decorative beauty,—its value as "pure design." That certain immutable laws of composition, determined by equally immutable properties of the human organism, are discoverable, and are to be implicitly obeyed by the artist, is an idea which seems to have found root in the East as far back as the fifth century. . . .

In many of the decorative effects of Japanese pictorial art, we find that certain forms of composition are used to an extent and with a skill not found elsewhere.

Balance in composition, for example, is more often attained by means of the principle of contrast than, as was usual with the Greeks, through a bilateral symmetry of design. A spot of dark is made to balance a light spot, rather than a similar spot of dark. . . .

Another device of the Oriental artist is to oppose one pattern, which is large but mild in effect, to another, which, though smaller, yet holds the attention with equal intensity by virtue of the stimulating character of its design, somewhat as a bright star offsets the softer beauty of the moon. Again, we often find two objects of unequal size made equally attractive to the eye, either by placing the smaller in greater isolation, or by treating it in greater detail; or else by informing it with greater interest. Sometimes, on the other hand, it is color rather than form or significance which preserves the balance. The red seal with which the Japanese painter signs his name often serves this purpose. Kiosai, when painting a picture of crows, is said to have spent three days in deciding where to place this important little red patch. There is yet another more subtle method employed for maintaining balance. Frequently the subject matter is placed in some corner of a picture, while the rest of the paper or silk remains bare. . . .

The constant employment of such varied methods of attaining harmony and equilibrium in composition permits a far greater variety of effect than where formal balance is alone used. This gives to Japanese art remarkable freshness and piquancy. Effects which in reality are the result of a very carefully planned scheme of composition seem due to happy accident. The color arrangements of the Japanese tend to emphasize this charm. For their color harmonies are subtle harmonies, special pleasure being taken in combining apparently irreconcilable color units into particularly beautiful color chords.

Ruskin but echoes the sentiment of all Japanese artists when he maintains that, in painting, the claim to immortality depends on the perfection and instantaneous precision of the single line. Line in the far East serves not one but many aesthetic ends. It is, as with us, greatly valued as an element of composition. The Japanese well understand that (as R. M. Stevenson puts it) "when you merely draw a line on an empty canvas you commit yourself to art, for you have given the line a positive character by placing it in some relation to the four sides of the canvas." A picture, indeed, is, as some one has said, in its beginning a pattern of lines; and the perfection in Eastern painting of "line combination" is unsurpassed.

Owing to the comparatively objective standpoint which the classic painter assumes toward his creation, one discovers, as a rule, little of the artist's personality. There is, however, one clue to the mind of the Japanese painter, and that is his line or brush-stroke. We all recognize how much of himself a man can express in his handwriting, even through that rigid implement, the pen. Imagine a case, however, where not the pen, but a much more delicate instrument, the brush, should be employed; let us further suppose a land where painting should grow out of a calligraphy already containing many aesthetic elements; and it will at once be seen that the special interest which attaches to line in writing—particularly writing of such a kind—would be transmitted to line in art.

Now in China, the fatherland of Japanese culture, the brush has been used from time immemorial as an instrument for writing as well as for painting. Moreover, for a long period calligraphy served the twofold function of providing aesthetic pleasure and recording thoughts; and later, when art evolved its own appropriate medium of expression, the interest and value attached to line as an ornament of handwriting was transferred to line as an instrument of pictorial art. In Japan, as in China, the great painter and the skilled calligraphist were often one and the same person. And to this day a bit of fine handwriting is treasured in the East as a work of art.

Further evidence of the importance which the Japanese attach to line is shown by the fact that a native connoisseur can pick from a large collection a given artist's work by an examination of this feature alone. Even the professional copyist of Japan, perhaps the most skillful in the world, is rarely able to imitate a famous painter's brush-stroke so as to deceive the expert.

As the personal quality of the line or brush-stroke reveals the individual, so also its general character denotes the school to which he belongs. For each school, at any rate to start with, evolved or borrowed from the Chinese that type of line which seemed best suited to the portrayal of its favorite class of subject. Thus the Tosa, Kano, and Sesshiu schools all had their characteristic brush-strokes. The quality of line, however, varied not merely with the school and individual, but with the nature of the details to be treated; one kind of line being used for the features, another for the dress, and so on. Great skill, moreover, was acquired in the representation of surface and texture by a varied handling of the brush. Artists like Shiubun, Sesshiu, and Tanyu could suggest to the sense of touch the feeling appropriate to the object depicted, by a sleight of hand so clever as to seem quite accidental.

Line as indicated by the brush has also been employed by the Oriental as a means of suggesting solidity, and as a substitute for light and shade. The drawing of Dürer, Rembrandt, and Holbein shows us how much can be accomplished in this respect by this simple method.

Many and various influences have caused the Japanese to prefer to suggest modeling, rather than elaborately to render it. In the first place, their mode of workmanship does not permit of the latter method. For their exclusive use of India ink and water color on such delicate and absorbent material as silk and Japanese paper renders alteration or the addition of many washes impracticable. Even more than in true fresco, effects must be produced directly and instantaneously. The chief reason, however, is undoubtedly an aesthetic one. The Japanese look upon painting as a form of decoration. Like the Greeks and Italians, and all who represent the classic spirit in art, they have always regarded the adornment of a household utensil, the decoration of a room, the painting of a "picture" as but various expressions of the same impulse,—the desire to beautify human life and its surroundings. For each of these branches of artistic effort, a certain difference of training may be needed, but ever the same faculty,—the decorative faculty. A Japanese picture, even though at first sight it seems but an "easel picture," and merely hangs against the wall, yet forms an essential part of its decorative scheme. A special alcove of suitable proportions is always provided for it. It is indeed true that a "Kakimono," as such a picture is called, is occasionally taken down, and another substituted, to suit the change of season, or the mood of its owner; but no Japanese who loves his pictures—and most of them do—would place in the "tokanoma," or alcove, one out of harmony with the general decorative effect. Needless to say, the paintings on the screens which form the partitions between rooms, and on those which stand detached, are essentially ornamental. As a decorative rather than a realistic intention is thus the primary one in Eastern painting, all elements, such as strong modeling by light and shade, which would disturb the decorative effect, are avoided.

That the Oriental has thus always followed the canons of what we call decorative art is, I think, fortunate. For it is these self-imposed limitations, which, by simplifying his problem, have enabled him to develop freely those beauties of line and line pattern, of dark and light "massing," and of color composition in flat tones, which have made his art famous throughout the West.

That decorative art should suggest to us certain limitations is a sign of our different aesthetic view-point. For the Japanese, while recognizing the realistic effect produced by the use of light and shade (and other similar devices), do not feel their omission as any serious artistic loss. To them painting is primarily a means of conveying emotion, not a method of reproducing natural fact. They regard it more as we do music. Hence the harmonies produced by a beautiful combination of lines and colors far outweigh in their opinion any pleasure which the feeling of being able to walk around and touch the objects in a picture can possibly confer. . . .

It seems hardly necessary to call attention to the skill with which the Japanese group and contrast flat masses of light and dark, colored or otherwise; for it is only a few years ago that our admiration of their tone harmonies (or Notan, as the Oriental terms this pictorial feature) resulted in the so-called "poster" movement. One might have supposed, judging from the sense of novelty and delight which these designs aroused, that some new principle of beauty had been discovered. The fact is, however, that one of the oldest and most important elements of pictorial art had been so long disregarded that its reappearance in a fresh form came as a revelation. We need only look beneath the surface to find this same principle of effect illustrated in the works of men like Raphael, Titian, Reynolds, and Millet. But people had come to dwell on so many other qualities in the work of such artists that they lost sight of this more fundamental one. It was reserved for Japan, whose art has been less burdened with the problems which the West has tried to solve, to bring clearly before us once more this form of beauty. . . .

The notion, too commonly entertained in the West, that what is most accurate in a scientific sense is necessarily the truest in an artistic, implies a confusion of ideas foreign to the clear-cut Japanese mind. It is not, therefore, surprising that the corollary of this Western fallacy, namely, that one impression of nature directly recorded is necessarily worth any number that are merely memorized, should be unsympathetic to their point of view. . . .

The Oriental artist does not so much seek to transcribe nature as to suggest her moods. His interest is centered in the poetic sentiment which she elicits. The saying of the Japanese, that a picture is a "voiceless poem," is particularly appropriate to their landscape painting. Our best artists also seek to express the poetry of nature. But they find it in many things. Our aesthetic pleasure in landscape is a complex one. The Oriental, on the other hand, in conformity with his type of mind, finds it in the dominant character,—in that which remains when all its accidents are eliminated; in other words, when it has been simplified and idealized. "For a landscape painting," to quote our Japanese critic once more, "is not loved because it is a facsimile of the natural scene, but because there is something in it greater than mere accurate representation of natural forms, which appeals to our feelings, but which we cannot express in words."

The Japanese landscape painter, therefore, as a general rule, is sparing of detail. We are sometimes inclined on this account to regard his completed work as nothing but a sketch. But to express more would be in his eyes to discredit the observer's perception and taste. For, as Mr. Lowell says, in his *Soul of the Far East,* "a full picture is as unsatisfactory to the Oriental as a long poem is to us. . . . It is the secret of great art to say much with little. . . ."

I have tried to suggest the attitude in which we may best approach Japanese painting, and to indicate some of its points of interest. I have intentionally refrained from dwelling on its peculiarities or defects. For they are self-evident. In fact, the sense of strangeness which must ever cling in a greater or less degree to Far Eastern art tends to make us overcritical toward it. Hence we are more apt to discover a lack of artistic ability in what is but the result of social and aesthetic forces acting under conditions unfamiliar to us, than to overlook any real deficiency. The common assumption that the apparent uniformity of Japanese art, as a whole, is due to a want of genuine artistic feeling, testifies to this fact. It is true that a lifeless formalism has at times marred Japanese painting; but this is not unnatural or surprising. It is, indeed, easy to see that all art which is imbued with the classic spirit incurs this risk. For, as the ideal of classicism is the attainment of the most finished, rather than the most original, result, the establishment of an aesthetic tradition or style is inevitable. But such a tradition is ever liable to abuse under the school system which it necessitates. For under such conditions the desire to preserve the tradition in all its purity is likely to be made an artistic end in itself. This, however, is simply saying that classicism, like any other artistic impulse, has its practical dangers and defects,— defects apparent not only in Japan, but in Greece, Italy, and France as well.

For the most part, however, the uniformity seen in Japanese, as in much Greek and later classic art, is but the mark of a definite style evolved by a school as the expression of its more permanent aesthetic convictions, and with which as a basis it effects those subtle alterations which gradually lead up to the perfect work of art.

We are often puzzled at our dissatisfaction with much of the modern decorative design, which under the name of *l'art nouveau* seeks a naturalistic effect similar to the Japanese. Yet to expect from such work a similar satisfaction is as reasonable as to look for Greek beauty in its modern imitation. The qualities which make Japanese design enduringly delightful are just those which require not years, but centuries, to develop. It is not the naturalism of Japanese decoration which is its greatest merit,—I have seen in Paris designs which showed a feeling for nature perhaps equally intimate. It is something more fundamental which gives to the Japanese product its distinct superiority. There is a peculiar unity of effect, a certain inner harmony of form, color, and design, unknown to the Western product.

The Japanese, with their natural, unsophisticated view of life, have ever sought in their art to mirror what a great painter and critic has termed "man's primordial predilections." Art, however, that seeks to embody pleasures founded on the unchanging properties of human nature, must have a past as well as a future, must be able to look backwards as well as forwards. Not one life's labor, but that of many generations, is required. No people have better understood this than the Japanese. They have also clearly perceived that no art that is not true to the changeless element in man can endure; while on the other hand any subject, however trivial, can be made eternally attractive, if only treated in accordance with aesthetic law.

Japanese painting delights us by its delicate fancy, its poetry, its freedom, its spirit; but what gives these qualities special and enduring charm,—what makes the play of fancy never wearisome, the liberty never mere license,—is that they find expression in and through a framework of design so finely conceived that therein we see reflected as in a mirror the fundamental principles which govern all true art.

5. THE EVOLUTION OF IMPRESSIONISM

OTTO STARK

In these days of strife between the impressionists and their opponents, it may not be amiss to look backward, and allow to pass in review, after a manner, the many changes which the movement has undergone, leading up to and culminating in modern color impressionism. This seems to me timely also from the fact that the meaning of the term appears to be either indefinite or perverted in the minds of a great number of those interested, both the sympathetic and the antagonistic. The Centennial Exposition at Philadelphia, with its art exhibition, can be considered as the real starting point of American art and impressionism in the modern sense, as through it a new ideal of the beautiful was established; or, at least a foundation was laid upon which to build. The display of foreign work in painting and sculpture, especially the former, opened the eyes of the American spectators to new things and methods, and doomed the then prevalent style and method of painting, of which Cropsey, Bierstadt, and others were the principal exponents, the Hudson River school, so called because never satisfied with the near-at-hand and simple, seeking the panoramic in landscape rather than the picturesque. Of figure painters, with a few notable exceptions, we had very few who were good, the tendency of nearly all their work and effort resulting in the dominion of cheap art. Who does not recall these pictures, flashy in color, smooth in painting, popular according to the successfulness with which they told a story, which, when a joke, was better still; figures painted without regard to surroundings and considered good when they were, as the popular phrase would have it, *finished,* which meant that the work was polished and "cooked up" in the best style.

With the Centennial, or shortly after it, however, came a revolution, brought about by some of our best students returning from abroad, or sending their work home. Munich men took

Modern Art, 3 (Spring, 1895), 54–56.

the lead, and the pictures and studies of such men as Chase, Duveneck and Shirlaw were a protest against the superficial, gaudy and unreal style then prevalent in American paintings. The marvelous technique, blackness (as we see and understand it now), love of simplicity in subject and treatment, breadth and vigor were a new revelation, and the "popular" painting could not withstand it long. The very faults of the Munich school were virtues, judged by the needs of the times. The blackness, for instance, was at times so pronounced that I well remember a saying, which became notorious in New York, of an artist who, standing before a water color by Currier, another of the American leaders of the period, which represented a road with trees silhouetted against a rainy sky, being asked what they were, answered, "Why, Ivory black of course"; and yet, this blackness and brownness had a mission to fulfill and did fill it, in bringing on a revolt against the wrong color sense of the period. But life means progress, and though the Munich movement had the effect of making us impatient with what it was a protest against, it nevertheless carried within itself that which was to doom it or make it only a round in the ladder of an upward movement in art, rather than a final achievement. A protest against it came very soon, in the so-called gray movement, brought mainly from France, and a more rigid method of drawing was sought after. The fine technique, simplicity and breadth of handling, was retained, but gray predominated as contrasted to the black and browns of the Munich method. This striving for grays was the result of the work carried on out of doors, or the "plein air" movement, which was making itself felt about that period.

This I consider the mightiest movement of modern times. With it came a new conception of nature, not confined to out-of-doors nature alone, for it very soon reacted also upon the work in the studio and in the house. Air and light were sought after as never before. The result of all this was shown in pictures, beautiful in repose, harmonious in tone, generally without shrill notes of any kind; good in values, in a monotone sense, but still lacking in light and colors. Working out of doors, painters could not help being attracted by sunlight, and serious attempts were made at rendering it. With this came still another movement, the so-called "high key" in painting, which meant to paint as light and as near white as the palette would allow, and well do I remember walking through exhibitions where a large percentage of canvases looked like white-washed fences, the paint being plastered on in a manner which reminded one of mortar put on with the trowel of a stone mason. Still it was not sunlight.

Gradually, working almost isolated, derided and scorned, came the present-day color impressionists. Their canvases began appearing, at first rarely, then more often, and now very often in the exhibitions. The conservatives protested, expostulated, became frantic and desperate in their efforts to stem the tide, but still it kept coming, gaining strength and new converts from year to year, until it had changed the aspect of our exhibitions as entirely as the sun changes night into day, and the conservatives themselves were against their will influenced by it. Finding, as the exhibitions became lighter and brighter, from season to season, their own work by contrast becoming correspondingly darker, they finally began to see that after all there was something worth studying in the new color movement. Very extravagant was, and still is, the work of the extremists; but we should not forget that revolutions are always brought about, in every department of human endeavor, not by those walking the middle road, but by extremists, and the difference between a crank and a reformer usually is, in the eyes of the majority, the difference between failure and success; though this rule can hardly be applied in discerning between a fashion, or a fad, and a revolution. This movement of color impressionism has proved itself to be a revolution by its staying qualities, and the influence it has had upon art and artists, as well as the public at large, in changing and leading forward many of our generation to a new idea of color, and opening their eyes to new beauties in nature, very often perhaps unconsciously. And while a great deal of the work done has been extreme, sacrificing everything to the qualities of color, movement, vibration and light, so that at times, at least, the uninitiated (and I suspect the supposed-to-be-initiated as well) could not tell which was top and which bottom of these pictures; yet the influence this work has had upon modern art, and especially American art, is hardly appreciated as yet. I consider that we are not at the end of it; beautiful work has been done, but still more beautiful is to come.

In visiting the art exhibition of the World's Fair, wandering through those innumerable galleries of paintings of all nations and peoples of the civilized world, I suddenly found myself in the rooms of the Swedish exhibit. I was almost overwhelmed with its strangeness. The effect it had upon me was like leaving a room or house filled with the polluted atmosphere caused by bad ventilation, and stepping out into the fresh air. My eyes were dazzled by the diffused light coming and surrounding me from all sides, and as I looked around, standing in the centre of each of these rooms, I saw that this group of painters (group I call them, because there were not many as compared to the great numbers represented from other countries) had attained as a number that which I had felt wanting in the works of most impressionists of other countries, a *complete color value,* or harmony of color. It seemed to me a realization of what others had been striving for, but as yet only successfully attained in single pictures or by single individuals; surely, I thought, one need have no especial education in art and painting to appreciate these. But speaking to my companions, who were not artists, I found that though they felt the same thrill of emotion in passing into this new revelation as I had, the beauty of these pictures, singly, was still hidden to them, that they still saw only crude colors where I saw beautiful impressions of nature. Then I fully realized what a change had overtaken me since the time when I would lie on my back on grassy slopes, with my head downwards, or look at nature with my head upside down, the art student's trick to see color exclusive of form.

The point I wish to make is this: I have found in nearly every case where impressionism is mentioned, that the word conveys an idea meaning color vibration, or crudity in color, to objectors, yet the word was used in an entirely different sense at the time of the Munich movement, so-called. Impressionists of that period were painters who worked in and searched for tone, quality and technique, painting in blacks and browns, colors being held in a low key. Those who, breaking loose from this blackishness and brownishness, worked in grays brought on by the "plein air" movement, were also called impressionists. Their impressionism consisted in striving to convey the diffused atmospheric light effects; harmony was one of the principal achievements, and value in the sense of monotone value. Impressionists again those were called who led in the "high key" or "white movement, and this finally leading up to the color movement, we have again impressionism; but this time in color.

As I look backwards it seems to me I see the movements following each other and classified by their hues and colors; at first the black or brown, next the gray, followed by white and finally by color, each distinct from the other, and yet one leading the way towards the other.

Impressionism to me has always meant the retaining of the first impression which nature makes upon us as we approach her, be it of tone, quality, harmony, light, vibration, force, delicacy, color, etc., and rendering this impression, if necessary, to the exclusion or at the sacrifice of details or other qualities and characteristics not so essential or vital, and rendering it unhampered by tradition and conventionalities.

What will be the next word is hard to say, unless it be individualism, and for American art Americanism. It seems to me I already see the beginning of a new move in this direction, and as everything genuine and of value is soon counterfeited, I can see in my mind the endless extravagances that will be indulged in by mediocrity under this name, choosing and following a method and movement not because understanding it, but because it is the order of the day.

Or is it not possible that if the present movement in color goes to seed, we may witness a reaction and see the experience of the last decade repeated on a higher plane?

However this may be, surely the strife will go on, and the hopeful part of it all is that strife means life and life is progress.

6. CLAUDE MONET

Claude Monet was born in Havre, and most of his life has
been passed in painting the river and valley of the Seine. He
knows that country well, by long explorations since his early
boyhood, on foot or in canoe—at all seasons of the year and
all hours of the day. And what a noble total of work he has
given the world, characterized from the first by an independence
of vision and uncompromising honesty, accompanied by an
unquenchable enthusiasm and love for his *motifs*.

A winter evening, the sun going down a red globe, gilding
cakes of floating ice; fog lifting, disclosing a mediæval village
with church and towers, fairy-like, wonderful; fields with ripen-
ing grain, bordered by gray-green trees; hill-sides with their
patchwork divisions, or with fruit-trees, blossom-covered; little
towns, their walls and houses reflected in the water, while a
long line of deep-laden barges passes slowly by; a river-side inn
frequented by yachtsmen, a gay mixture of boats, brilliant costumes and flags, the whole twinkling and dancing in the rippling
water; islands gorgeous with autumn coloring—these are a few
glimpses in the long panorama evoked by the painter's magic.

In the "View of Rouen," with what directness and justness
of vision has a *chef-d'œuvre* been created! Everything moves
and vibrates in the delicious summer air, the little boats rock
gently at anchor, the tall poplars nod, and clouds sail across the
luminous sky. One likes his work of this period for its youth and
gayety; never has landscape painting, unhampered by non-
essentials, spoken so directly to the heart of the charm of nature
and the joy of living.

Scribner's Magazine, 19 (January, 1896), 125.

7. CURRENT IMPRESSIONISM

LOUIS WEINBERG

Impressionism in art is something more than a method of painting. Although intimately interwoven in its origin with discoveries in the physics of light, it became the dominant school of the last few decades through no mere chance coincidence of a Chevreul and a Monet. For impressionism has a broader significance and a truer one than is expressed in the technical formulae of its painter disciples, with their broken color tones, their purer palette, their interest in values, in luminous shadows and in vibrating light. Its principles have strongly marked the novel, the short story, the poem, the drama, the statue and the symphony. Its meaning and the causes for its ascendancy must be sought in the very character of the life which it so well reflects.

Impressionism as a technique is a means of recording the transitory nature of phenomena and the fluidity of motion. As a principle it is based on a philosophy of change. As painters, as writers, as musicians, impressionists are not so much men of strong convictions and deep words as they are craftsmen recording the flitting sensations of an ever changing world. The chief interest of impressionism is the ephemeral.

But this is not alone a description of the art of our times. It is the very essence of our lives. We move in an age of impressionistic living. All is atmosphere and movement. There are relatively few hard contours, all is a matter of environment. There are few fundamental bed-rock traditions or deeply rooted faiths. Most things are enveloped in the vibrating atmosphere of doubt—light, the rationalists call it. In our social life, in our industrial life, in our political and in our very religious life, all is change. In place of the old social castes we still have a constant shifting of social planes. The mechanic travels from city to city, from trade to trade. Creed follows creed, party follows party, and in the confused panorama of varying policies, a policy well drawn and classic in proportion is hardly to be expected.

New Republic, 2 (March 6, 1915), 124–25.

To this mode of living and thinking, science, which through the industrial revolution had contributed so much to the building up of the new social order, now adds still further kaleidoscopic variety. The railroad, the telephone, the telegraph, the linotype machine, the steamship, the phonograph and "the movies," all contribute to the rush of changing impressions, to the bewildering multiplicity of effects. What time is there for revery, imagination or principle in the life of the modern city dweller? His newspaper furnishes numberless thrills each hour. His library is a storehouse of electric sensations and impressions. His very excursions and vacations are not given to idling or to play. They are arranged on compact tourist schedules. Torn between a thousand sensations he grows sensation-sated. To hold his interest the impressionist statesman, churchman, play producer, manufacturer, and publisher each vie with one another in providing new sensations and fresh thrills.

The dominance of impressionism in our art is the outcome of this life. The motive of this aesthetic creed is not expression or the search for beauty, it is curiosity. The interest of life is in each moment; of nature, in its slightest quivering tone; of humanity, in the least gesture of its meanest citizen. In landscape the play and constantly varying quality of light constitute its message. The special technique is merely the outcome of this vision. Form and line are lost in veils of atmosphere, vibration is suggested by the broken color tones of a spectrum palette, and luminosity by the pitch and color of the shadows. In figure painting, movement as well as the play of light is recorded. The clear-cut divinities of Poussin's "Arcadia" make way for the laundress, the barmaid, the jockey and the ballet dancer. In place of the old gods living in their classic world of static calm, restless moving throngs on balconies and busy boulevards now greet the vision of the art lover.

Your impressionist painter does not depict fundamental passions, death, love, hate, revenge or lust. He is anti-sentimental and opposed to the literary. He paints the passing moment, extolling its rapidly departing beauty. His workmen are not actors in the drama of toil refashioning the world. His peasants are not like Millet's, statuesque men spiritualized or brutalized by contact with a stubborn soil. They are moving color spots bathed in atmosphere. As the laundresses of Degas stand over their boards, they reveal the hitherto unobserved interest of a characteristic attitude; their wash reflects the cool light, their faces are free from sentiment. Renoir's boatmen are not heroes of the sea; they are bits of humanity as evanescent as the atmosphere. The queer little shove with which they launch their boats upon the water is noted with sensitive feeling for the fluid pose of the body. The figures flit across the artist's stage in much the same manner that wind plays through the meadows and light reflects from window panes. Poe speaks of the drama of life in which the hero is man, the conqueror death. Here the hero is light and the conqueror change. But the dramatic element must be added by the commentator. Impressionism is truly the product and expression of the spirit of its day. It is modern not because it depicts the *demi-mondaine* and the ballet girl, the factory and the railroad yard. It is modern because it is born of the new sensitiveness to the passing moment.

In literature the development and vogue of the short story is the product of impressionism, although the novel and the drama have been strongly influenced. Our journalism is almost all cheaply impressionistic; not principle but curiosity is the main motive; gossipy impressions of fleeting events, talky reviews of ephemeral books, an endless array of snapshots of people and places momentarily in the public eye. Our very criticism is impressionistic and without standards. Just as an impressionist painter wanders from effect to effect, so does the impressionist critic survey the new novel, drama or painting. It hath such and such an look to me, he tells us in a style more or less bantering; and the interest of the criticism lies quite obviously not in the convictions of the writer, but in the manner in which he records his own passing impressions. When serious thought expressed itself with academic pedantry, this new criticism entered with the same delightful charm as did the short story of Kipling into the land of Meredith. But the stale freshness of the reviewer tires one. There is a joy in an idea that can never be felt any more in the "fresh" statements of inconsequential nothings.

To-day there are those who look upon the entrenched principle of impressionism as an obstacle in the way of growth. They revolt against its tyranny. Impressionism is subject to decay by its own law, the law of change. The mental attitude which expressed itself in impressionism has lost its freshness. Although they once had a certain charm and brought a message of keener observation and more sensuous living, these gossipy notes no longer appeal. In painting, the "modern" movements in art were partly a reaction to the febrile note of impressionism. To the impressionistic insistence on atmosphere was opposed a new feeling for the architectonic, for the plastic form. There was an endeavor to free art from the restraint of formulae largely scientific and optic, so that it could express a fuller imaginative vision. The artist is not a sensitive physicist with a brush in his hand enslaved to a given palette; he is not a recorder of given values arising out of the chance tones of the moment. He need obey no laws but those of artistic necessity. His color values should be emotional values. His composition should be synthetic, controlled by decorative requirements or by expressive effectiveness and not by the "agreeable surprise" of accidental grouping.

Not only among these experimenters and searchers but even among the lay lovers of art the number is growing of those who are wearied by all the goodly gossips and their kind catering. This army of dissenters are no longer satisfied with impressionist portrayers of passing moments; they seek expressionists, depicters of the significant, less concerned with atmosphere than with the form, the more enduring substance, which it envelops. While it cannot be denied that change is the law of life and that for the artist there must be unending interest in the fleeting aspects of nature, art would grow in dignity, just as criticism, politics and journalism, just as life itself would, if it were less indiscriminately curious, a little more inclined to discover for itself the significant in the drift of the fleeting and the ephemeral.

8. THE LESSON OF THE PHOTOGRAPH

KENYON COX and RUSSELL STURGIS

The time in which we are living might well be known as the age of photography. It is at least possible to believe that of all the wonderful discoveries or inventions of the nineteenth century that of photography is the most important, and that it will prove more far-reaching in its effects than any other since the invention of printing. The invention of printing was the discovery of a method for the preservation and multiplication of the record of human thought; the invention of photography was the discovery of a method for the obtaining, the preservation, and the multiplication of records of fact. Printing can only record what man knows or thinks; photography can record many things which man does not know and has not even seen, much less understood. In photography there is no personal equation. What a man has photographed is different from what he has seen or thinks he has seen, from what he declares he saw, from what he draws. Within its limits it is an accurate statement of what was. Hence, photography is one of the most valuable of the tools of science, at once a means of research and an invaluable, because impersonal, record. Its applications are infinite, and we are probably only at the beginning of them. It has become the indispensable tool not only of the natural sciences, but of everything that touches upon science, of every study in which fact is of more importance than opinion or feeling. It will make history something different in the future from what it has been in the past, and, by the multiplication of reproductions of works of art, it has already revolutionized art-criticism.

But what has been and what is likely to be the influence of this great invention upon art itself? It has certainly added in some ways to the education of the artist; as an implement of investigation it has taught us much about the science of natural aspects. Yet, up to the present, its influence would seem to have been evil rather than good. We have had painters trying to rival

Scribner's Magazine, 23 (May, 1898), 637–40.

the photograph in its accuracy of statement, and so nearly succeeding that their work has been hardly distinguishable from
that of the camera, and now we have the camera attempting in
its turn to produce art. Many of the cheaper magazines are
illustrated almost wholly by photography, and nowadays they
are filled with what are known as "photographic art-studies,"
and we have whole exhibitions of the same sort of thing, like
a recent one at the Academy of Design. One might almost be
forgiven for thinking that art and photography have grown so
to resemble each other that the mere cheapness and facility of
the latter is destined to win the day for it, without regard to its
superiority in verisimilitude, and that photography is likely, in
the near future, entirely to supplant art.

There are, however, other signs of the times which point to
an entirely opposite conclusion. Are not these the days, or
rather, was not yesterday the day, of the poster fad? The poster
is as far as possible from photographic; has as little as possible
to do with fact or nature; is, in its extremest form, pure decoration run mad. Yet the day of the poster is coincident with the
day of the photograph. The crisis of that fever is passed, but look
at the current numbers of the "up-to-date" art-periodicals and
observe the dominance of personality in the work they pub-
lish and comment upon, its decorativeness, its subjectivity, the
variety of "tendencies" and "movements," of *alitys* and *isms,*
that are represented. Never have there been so many schools
and groups and secessions. Impressionists and symbolists and
the Rose + croix, tonalists and colorists and luminists, are rampant. In art this is preeminently a period of anarchy and revolt,
and the revolt is precisely against the photograph and the photographic, though it has seemed at times that the revolutionaries
would batter down many good things also, including sound
drawing and common-sense.

No, the real danger at present is hardly that art will submit
to the sway of photography, but that it will go too far in its
rebellion and forget truth as well as mere fact. For photography
is hopelessly ugly. The dreariness of the "photographic art-
study" which has so impressed the artist, will end by impressing

the public, and even the multitude will, in the long run, resent being fobbed off with mere nature when they ask for art.

If photography teaches the world nothing else, it will teach it that the end of art is not imitation. It will never again be possible for a great artist to believe, as Leonardo believed, that his aim is the production of a picture resembling as nearly as possible the reflection of nature in a mirror. We have the reflection made permanent all about us, and it does not suffice. The photograph has killed the doctrine of "realism." But neither will the old doctrine of "idealism" answer any longer. The realist taught that you should paint nature as it is, the idealist that you should paint nature as it ought to be. But the photograph shows us that nature is no more like Rembrandt than like Raphael, and that the something which is art exists in the work of Terburgh as unmistakably as in that of Titian, while it does not exist in nature itself or in the impersonal record of nature. What is this something? The shortest word for it is arrangement. It is some form of order, harmony, proportion. It is arrangement of line, arrangement of color, arrangement of light and shade, for the sake of forming a harmoniously ordered whole which shall express some phase of human emotion and satisfy some vague desire of the human heart. There is even an arrangement of graven lines or of the strokes of a brush, so that "mere technique" may also be artistic and have its reason in the creation of harmonies, though they be not harmonies of the highest order of importance. Sometimes nature fortuitously arranges itself into a semblance of pictorial harmonies, and sometimes a photograph may seize and perpetuate one of these accidental arrangements, and then we have the best that photography can give us. The "snap-shot" at a landscape under a fine effect, or at the momentary grouping of figures in movement, is often deeply interesting to artists, although it is not art. But the more consciously the photographer attempts to be an artist the worse, in general, are his results, because the complicated harmonies which the painter arranges on his canvas are impossible of achievement anywhere else. You cannot pose figures as painters pose them, nor arrange drapery as they arrange it. You cannot get real light to fall as it falls in pictures, or natural color to

harmonize as pictorial color harmonizes. The artist's arrangement is complete, each smallest detail fitted to its place in the
whole, each line and each touch of color studied and modified
until its relation with every other line and every other touch is
perfect, and these relations, although infinitely subtle and complex, are subject to unascertained mathematical law as certainly
as the relations of notes in a musical score are subject to a
law better known and partially understood. Try to pose figures
before the camera and to make a picture like some work of art
that you have seen, and you will discover that it cannot be done.
If one detail is right, another will be wrong. The painter has
studied the parts separately, trying again and again for this line
or that shade until everything fills its allotted place in a comprehensive scheme; but the photographer must get them all right
at once or not at all. The result is that deadest of pictures,
the *tableau vivant*.

We all see photographs to-day, and most of us take them,
and from this fact must surely come, if not a knowledge of what
art is, at least a more general knowledge than has ever before
existed in the world of what it is *not*. But while art is arrangement and not imitation, in the art of painting the things to be
arranged are the forms and colors of nature. The art may be
good while the representation is poor, but there is no reason why
the art should not be finer while the representation is truer. If
the artist's knowledge is not so great that he can mould nature
to his harmony, then he must leave the nature out, for the
harmony is the essential; but if the harmony is attained, then
the more nature is included in it the more delightful is the art.
The figure-designer should know the human figure so well that
he can fit it to any scheme of line without ever a bit of false
anatomy, and there is surely no reason why the landscape-
painter should not be able to produce great harmonies of color
and tone without one misstatement of nature's laws of light. For
the competent artist there is no more necessity of falsification
than there is need that the poet should write nonsense because
he writes in verse. Meanwhile, there are no fully competent
artists, and we need demand of those we have only that they shall

be composers first, and that afterward they shall give us as much nature as they have learned to control.

Such is the lesson of the photograph. If we learn it, the influence of photography upon art will have been for good and not for evil.   K. C.

As K. C. says, and as his words still more strongly imply, the photograph has been sent us especially to teach the public what art is, that is to say, the art of the painter and the sculptor. The prodigious difference between the artist's representation of any natural object and the photograph of that same object is something which does not strike us so forcibly as we look at a drawing made by some monochrome process, but is very evident when it is the photograph which is before us. And yet there is a distinction to be drawn and a question to be asked with regard to it.

The photograph of a landscape subject is often of such refinement, "composing" so well, and affording so graceful and attractive a picture, that the public may be excused for asking if that is not landscape-art; and even the student may be allowed to ask the same pertinent question. A picture of a distant mountain-peak made as some out-of-door photographers know how to make it, has a delicacy of tint, a subtlety of line, reproducing something of that strange passing of the mountain into the sky which the student of nature knows but which beats the painter's efforts to render. And if, as will constantly happen, the mountain is much more gradual in its slopes and much less "alpine" in character in the photograph than we, in our excitement, looking at it, had supposed it to be; and if it is to be supposed that the painter would have falsified these slopes and that highest acclivity in order to tell more strongly the story of the mountain, as by a sort of exaggeration which is of the same nature as caricature, then it is a question at once whether such exaggeration be not a barbarous and primitive resort of the painter's art—whether the great mountain-painter ought not to find mountain character without so childish a device as that piece of falsification. Even the recollection of Turner's practice and the weight of his great authority leaves one in a questioning mood about this important matter. Or, to take the more familiar instance of the hedgerow, the stile, and the turning of the lane in English landscape, or the familiar group of cows under a tree, or of poplars by the side of still water, or of children in a blackberry patch, the landscape being the essence of the picture in each case, there is many an instance of this sort of photographic picture which is very attractive even to the artist familiar to weariness with the drawings of a thousand masters who have gone before. And yet even Mr. Ruskin, best known to us all as worshipper of nature and preacher against conventions of art, tells his readers that the photographers ought to spend their strength on the perishing ancient buildings of Europe, remembering always that a photograph of a landscape is but a toy, while a photograph of a fine ruin is a document of precious significance.

In Florence, twenty years ago, a student of architecture was buying photographs on a rather large scale, when a painter of his acquaintance, and a devout follower of Ruskin's teachings, asked him how he could bear to spend money on such inartistic things as photographs. The answer was easy, relating as it did exclusively to photographs of architecture, sculpture, and objects of decorative art—it was that a photograph was a mere glass through which one saw the veritable object which he wished to study. The artistical character was not in the photographic picture, but in the object which it reproduced. Through the ugly purplish brown of a silver-print more of the truth concerning the church front, "set full for the sun to shave," was visible than could be seen through any drawing over which he, the artist, might have spent long summer afternoons. This is the essence of the photograph, that it preserves every record, with some drawbacks and shortcomings, of what is put before it. If that thing is artistic, the photograph, in an indirect and secondary way, becomes itself artistic, as the reflection of a man's face in a glass is the man himself; so far and no farther. There are some scraps of landscape which the artist can hardly improve upon in grace or in severity of composition. What is it that a critic says of the picture by Corot which he actually saw in process of being painted? Something to this effect: that at first he could not see what Corot, with his canvas out-of-doors in the forest of Fontainebleau, was trying to do, even the half-finished picture on the easel not fixing the subject sufficiently for the inquirer's information, until suddenly he saw, eighty yards away, in the dim middle distance, Corot's picture rising out of the ground. Corot, the least realistic of out-of-door painters, the most determined of all men to give one, and usually the same, familiar impression—the deliberate painter at noonday of dawn-effects and of twilight skies—Corot could yet plant himself in front of a composition ready made for him and modify it only in part as he worked. What, then, does the skilled and artistically intelligent photographer do? He selects the Corot subject, and, as he cannot alter it, he selects it with even more patient care. And what is his result? It is a transcript of a piece of nature which the photograph-artist has thought the most lovely within his immediate reach. It is not a work of landscape-art, but of skill and taste in choosing landscape. The photographer, tied to the veritable facts before him, must select with more patient and longanimous care than the landscape-painter, or he has achieved nothing whatever.

So much for landscape; but then it is notorious that real landscape comes nearer to our ideal landscape than some other manifestations of nature do to our ideal of them. To go at once to the other extreme, to the very opposite pole of the artistic world, how about figure-drawing, and especially the nude? Has anyone ever seen a photograph of the nude or semi-nude model, no matter how admirably chosen or how artistically posed, which was not really ugly when considered from the point of view of the trained observer of drawings of the figure? Rembrandt was not much of a chooser of models, at least in the direction of their loveliness, and there are not many uglier individuals in the great gallery of nude figures than the Adam and the Eve in his magnificent etching, and yet these two figures are lovely when compared with the photograph of the nude model. And the reason for this is clearly that the conventions of art—the accepted conventions of art—the conventions upon which all our ideas of figure-painting and figure-drawing are based—are all an ideal very remote indeed from the actual fact. Consider a Greek statue of a perfectly central type, neither early nor late, neither primitive nor of the decline—consider the Hermes found fifteen years ago at Olympia, and made popular by the numerous casts of its bust and the numerous photographs of the whole figure. Neither in actual modelling of the smaller parts nor in the texture of surface is this much like the nude body even of the most athletic, the most healthy, the most admirably "trained" male model. The splendid young men whom one sees at the swimming-bath, they too, the fine-drawn and highly bred youths of our best races, and in admirable physical condition, are so unlike the Greek statue, that one looks once and again with amazement, asking whether this indeed is the origin of the Greek convention.

It is notorious that many of our living masters of the human form in painting, use the model only occasionally. It would not be hard to make a considerable list of men who, by their own confession, or by the statements of their friends, are known to compose and even to draw in detail without consulting the model at all, using the model afterward to correct their work, or, perhaps, in case of a long-lasting toil, referring to it more than once in the course of their work. Some of these artists have, indeed, posed the separate models for their separate figures in advance, first nude and then afterward draped. But there are those who will tell you that this plan is dangerous, because it leads to immobility, and to a look given to the figures in the final work as if they could not move, but were statues draped and colored. This is not the place to discuss these delicate subjects at length, but they should be in the mind of every one who looks at photographs of human subject and asks in what consists their extraordinary lack of artistic value. The draped figure follows at some distance the nude figure in all these conditions and conventions of art. The instantaneous photograph alone can give it movement and the charm of seeming alive; but at what a cost of grace!—at what a cost of artistic interest! Mr. Muybridge's photographs of man, beast, and bird in rapid motion are invaluable as documents, but we have yet to hear of the enthusiast who shall admire them as possessions in the sense that a work of art is a possession.   R. S.

III

The Public Arts

Growing cities offered the most striking evidence of industrialism's centralizing tendencies. Lacking a traditional urban life-style, however, most Americans found cities bewildering. They felt uncomfortable with congestion in a country renowned for spaciousness. A fragmented system of government inhibited quick public action to prevent or control urban problems. And a deeply ingrained individualistic ethic clashed with the need for communal action and expenditure.

But the traditional American aversion to governmental planning that affected private property gave way slowly to community needs. Civic groups and important individuals often led in seeking parks, zoned areas, and public beautification. The results were dramatic in many places. New York City's Central Park was a suitable memorial to its planner, Frederick Law Olmstead. Daniel Burnham, architect and planner, rationalized and decorated part of Chicago's lakefront and marina. The federal capitol in Washington underwent extensive beautification and rebuilding after 1902. Every major city boasted plazas, boulevards, and public buildings directed at satisfying a desire for grandeur. Areas devoted to public activities underwent closer planning than those meant for private living; government could provide attractive and elevating environments for communal events. "The City Beautiful Idea," created in an international style derived from historic Old World models, became a subject of public discussion and action.

Sculptors acquired a welcome prominence, generally opting for an allegorical realism that emphasized the nation's great men and historic past. Monumental portrait sculpture culminated in the massive seated likeness of Abraham Lincoln that Daniel Chester French created for the Lincoln Memorial. There was a general desire for symbolic portrait statuary to emphasize individual deeds in an age when individuals seemed to shrink in importance. And nearly every town graced a park with a monument to the Civil War dead. Sculpture was changed from an essentially private form, the concern of museums and a few wealthy collectors, into a public art.

Augustus Saint-Gaudens (1848–1907), trained in Paris and imbued with his country's idealism, quickly became the era's most famous American sculptor. He avoided the smooth, lifeless marble surface so dear to classically inspired sculptors for a warm, rough bronze texture that made his figures seem to be snapshots in motion. His greatest statues entered the public consciousness, symbolizing heroic values without losing sight of the individual involved. His most famous works were probably the Lincoln statues; the winged victory leading General Sherman; and a magnificent statue of Admiral David Farragut. Saint-Gaudens was equally famous for medallions, bronze plaques, and memorial figures such as that for Henry Adams' wife in Washington, D.C. He also designed a new U.S. coinage in 1905.

Though mural painting had an ancient lineage, it was popular and vital only twice in American history. During the 1930s the government employed artists to decorate public buildings. And the form acquired sudden prominence during the Gilded Age. This impetus reflected the era's concern both for display, and for education. Critics and commentators saw wall paintings, whether in public or private buildings, as a didactic form. Their decorative quality would soften the materialism of a bank or hotel lobby, would dignify activities in public buildings, and would ennoble observers. Most muralists were figure painters, who relied on allegory and classical examples.

Varied desires fueled the concern for monumentality and public decoration. City crowding and squalor certainly needed offsetting. The "higher ideals" in stone and bronze would uplift both tenement and brownstone dwellers. Formal architecture also emphasized a desire for attachments to tradition, and for unity with world tastes. All together revealed the Republic's power and promise.

9. SAINT-GAUDENS'S LINCOLN

M. G. VAN RENSSELAER

The Lincoln monument for Chicago is the most important commemorative work that Mr. St. Gaudens has yet produced and may well remain the most important of his life. There could be no nobler task for an American sculptor than the task of representing the greatest of all Americans; and it so chances that the external as well as the intellectual problems it involved were of peculiar interest and difficulty.

To an artist brought up in the belief that only through the representation of purely beautiful forms can a work of sculpture be beautiful as such, Lincoln would, of course, have offered an unsympathetic theme; both in physical structure and in attire he might have seemed almost the embodiment of the sculpturally impossible. But to an artist trained like Mr. St. Gaudens in the gospel of individuality, full of that modern spirit which prizes "character" in a model for portraiture above even beauty

Century Magazine, 35 (November, 1887), 37–39.

itself, no face could have been more inspiring than Lincoln's, while even the difficulties presented by his form and costume could not seem insuperable.

The intellectual problem on the other hand—the primary task of conceiving the soul and potency of the man is so clear and full a way as to make adequate expression possible—had to deal with elements in which force and beauty were equally commingled. A more distinct personality than Lincoln's could not be imagined, nor one in which moral purity and power should be more commensurate with intellectual strength. Here it was the complex richness of his opportunity which made the sculptor's task as difficult as noble. We may truly say that Lincoln was not one great man but many. He was a thinker whose profound imaginings dealt with the deepest, subtilest public problems and a practical man of affairs who controlled a myriad of daily details of immediate definite bearing; a leader who guided his people through a terrible crisis, yet an executive who carefully sought out and followed out their own desires; the champion of his country before the world and the father individually of every fellow-countryman who appealed to him; a wonderful orator and a wonderful master of prose expression and of the poetry which may be woven into it; a humorist and yet a philosopher saddened by the ever-present pathos and tragedy of life. His mind seemed a very synonym for practical good sense; yet it was the mind of a poet, a prophet too, and beneath it lay the heart of a child and the tender instincts of a woman. How, we had often asked ourselves, can any artist ever show us such a character? And how can we permit him to dismember it and accept a single part as Lincoln? Yet Mr. St. Gaudens has not dismembered it, and has expressed it for us no less adequately than broadly.

The first question to be decided must have been: Shall the impression to be given base itself primarily upon the man of action or upon the man of affairs? Shall the statue be standing or seated? In the solution of this question we find the most striking originality of the work. The impression given bases itself in equal measure upon the man of action and the man of affairs. Lincoln is standing, but stands in front of a chair from which

he has just risen. He is before the people to counsel and direct
them, but has just turned from that other phase of his activity
in which he was their executive and their protector. Two ideas
are thus expressed in the composition, but they are not separately, independently expressed to the detriment of unity. The
artist has blended them to the eye as our own thought blends
them when we speak of Lincoln. The pose reveals the man of
action, but represents a man ready for action, not really engaged
in it; and the chair—clearly typical of the Chair of State—reveals
his title to act no less than his methods of self-preparation.

We see, therefore, that completeness of expression has been
arrived at through a symbolic, idealistic conception. No given
moment of Lincoln's life is represented, no special branch of
his public usefulness or of his intellectual endowment is emphasized,—all are suggested in the symbolic reach of the conception.
But the rendering of his conception is realistic in the best sense
of the word. The pose is simple, natural, individually characteristic—as far removed from the conventionally dramatic or
"sculpturesque" as from the baldly commonplace. Neither physical facts nor facts of costume are palliated or adorned. Even
the chair is in general outline such a one as Lincoln might very
possibly have used. It is idealized only by its massiveness and
its unobtrusive decoration, and the figure is idealized only by
refinement and breadth and vigor in treatment. What we see are
realities, but we see them suffused with poetic thought and typical explanatory meanings, and ennobled though not altered by
the subtile touch of art: and the reposeful composition speaks
to us with true dramatic intensity. Examine the figure more
narrowly and see how rich it is in significance, how it carries
out in every line the fundamental ideas which inspired the composition as a whole. This Lincoln, with his firmly planted feet,
his erect body, and his squared shoulders, stands as a man accustomed to face the people and sway them at his will, while the
slightly drooped head and the quiet, yet not passive hands express the meditativeness, the self-control, the conscientiousness
of the philosopher who reflected well before he spoke, of the
moralist who realized to the full the responsibilities of utterance.
The dignity of the man and his simplicity; his strength, his

inflexibility and his tenderness; his goodness and his courage; his intellectual confidence and his humility of soul; the poetic cast of his thought, the homely vigor of his manner, and the underlying sadness of his spirit,—all these may be read in the wonderfully real yet ideal portrait which the sculptor has created. And they are all so expressed, I repeat, as to reveal not only the man himself but the various directions in which he brought his great qualities to bear.

Having said as much as this, it is almost needless to comment upon the technical merits of the work. No such meaning, no such message could have made itself felt through any but the most accomplished hand. When we find for the first time a portrait which really shows us the inner Lincoln we are not surprised to find it the first one which from a purely sculptural point of view has dealt successfully with his outward aspect. This aspect was impressive, imposing, inspiring, attractive by reason of the spirit which shone through it; and, naturally, an artist who failed to reveal that spirit could make little of the rough yet noble husk which sheathed it. The lesson thus taught is a priceless one. It proves that even the most difficult task of the most "modern" kind is not beyond the power of the sculptor's art to master; but that it can only be mastered when that art signifies intellectual insight and creative force as well as trained perceptions and a skillful hand.

Another valuable lesson may be read in the nature of that originality which I have claimed for the design as a whole. Strange as it may seem, no previous monumental composition had furnished a precedent for this. The world had had seated statues and standing statues in plenty; but a figure thus recently risen from its seat is that rarest of things—a true novelty in art. No novelty in art, however, is entitled to admiration simply as such. On the contrary, it is trebly bound to make manifest intrinsic worth. We cannot but criticise it with senses sharpened by the thought: If the idea is good, would not some great artist long ere this have conceived it and expressed it? The exceptional strength of Mr. St. Gaudens's talent shows not so much in the originality of his fundamental idea as in that treatment of it which has made it seem not merely a right idea but the only one adequate to his purpose. This implies, of course, that originality came not because it was sought as such, but naturally, inevitably, as a result of the conscientious effort to express a clear conception in the clearest and completest way.

In conclusion, it is most interesting to note the close ties which connect so original, individual a work as this with other great works of other kinds. The union of idealistic conception and realistic rendering which it reveals is almost always found when modern art is at its very best. But it also shows a union of perfect repose with strong dramatic significance, and this union is characteristic of classic art when at its best. There as here it is secured by the same expedient,—by the choice of a moment which is not the one of most vigorous action but the one in which such action is imminent.

The statue is of bronze, eleven and a half feet in height. The simple pedestal which supports it stands in the center of a platform some sixty feet in breadth by thirty in depth which is raised a few steps above the surface of a slight elevation near the entrance of Lincoln Park. Around three sides of the platform curves a stone seat upon the back of which one reads the name of Lincoln, with the dates of his birth and death, and upon the ends two characteristic citations from his own utterances. In the architectural portion of his work Mr. St. Gaudens was assisted by Mr. Stanford White, and together they have given us a monument which is the most precious the country yet possesses; which is not only our best likeness of Abraham Lincoln, but our finest work of monumental art.

10. THE OUTLOOK FOR DECORATIVE ART IN AMERICA

FRANK FOWLER

. . . . .

From the few instances given of decorative work already produced by us, it will be seen that we have reached a point in building when, in the houses, hospitals, churches, hotels, theatres, colleges, and courts of justice that are projected, the growing needs of the people require something more than the adaptability of plan to the purpose it serves. In a word, we have passed the period in architecture of accepting only what is necessary, and we now demand that our taste shall be consulted in the matter. We have been strictly utilitarian long enough, and there is a present disposition on the part of the public to go beyond the obviously practical in the art of building, and to recognize the practicality of appealing to the mind. This is a great step, and it is full of encouragement.

Although I do not say that our artists have, as yet, given us largely of the decorative quality—mainly, perhaps, for lack of opportunity—still I am convinced that they have never before been so well equipped to do so. The discrimination in presenting what is most salient and typical, while leaving realistic studies for the portfolio, is taking art out of the sphere of the pictorial and definite, and into the realm of the imaginative and suggestive. The sentiment of things, and not the things themselves, is what vivifies, stimulates and inspires. Each man then becomes individual; he does not reproduce, he interprets; and in the proportion that his mental gifts are superior, in just that degree you will mark superiority in his art.

Now it is this power of abstraction, so valuable, and indeed so essential in all decorative composition, which makes the expression *"le grand art"* in France a synonym for decoration, and its pursuit and practice there of the highest importance. Let us concede then, that until the present we have had no intimation

The Forum, 18 (February, 1895), 686–93.

of a "grand art," but have limited ourselves to easel work and
an occasional historical subject or panoramic landscape. Artists
here for more reasons than one have been somewhat slow in
approaching this broader field. Perhaps the greatest immediate
obstacle to the production of work on a large scale is the lack
of space to exhibit canvases of great extent. If an artist feels a
subject in heroic proportions he has no incentive to attempt it,
for he knows that the opportunity to exhibit a composition of
unusual size is practically *nil*. In France one is not handicapped
by such considerations. Sixty or one hundred feet of space will
be given there to a work, should this be necessary, if it possess
sufficient merit to be shown at all. I have known brilliant young
men, so poor that they were obliged to paint, to sleep, and to
take most of their meals in the close quarters of their studios,
who would stretch a canvas to the full limits at their disposal—
perhaps twenty-five by fifteen feet—project upon it some biblical, mythological, or historical composition, and put a year of
earnest work on its production, economizing closely to defray
the expenses of materials and models, knowing that when finished it would not be excluded from the spacious walls of the
Palais de l'Industrie on the score of dimensions merely. It is
only too obvious that lack of exhibition space is one cause, and
an important one, why we have attempted so little of the kind
of work that is an essential preparation for the even greater
achievement of mural design. If it were possible to secure some
building, of the area of Madison Square Garden in New York,
for instance, in which to hold an annual exhibition of the fine
arts, the stimulus given to mural painting and works of importance tending in that direction would undoubtedly be great. I
feel confident that ambitious painters would take heart if assured
of exhibition room, and that subjects which they feel "*en grand*"
would be produced by them in consequence of this assurance.

It is the business of the decorator, the mural painter, to bear
in mind, when working in restricted quarters as he frequently
does, the position in which his painting is to be ultimately seen.
If he fails to do this he fails in all, so far as the decorative quality
of his work is concerned; and it is only in an exhibition hall of
ample proportions that the result may be judged with fairness.

There are many painters who do not care to confine themselves wholly to easel pictures; and it is doubtless true that with adequate provision for the exhibition of heroic canvases or large mural motives and designs, these would be forthcoming, to the inevitable enrichment of our art. For it is on the lines of decoration that a high standard of drawing is maintained, a great breadth and simplicity of painting demanded, and that splendid power of deduction and synthesis called for which divests the forms of nature of all that is not inherently large and noble. It is thus that the highest qualities of art are conserved and protected from the littlenesses which, in its more restricted practice, too often creep in to degrade. For this class of work calls upon the painter to reject or to choose from that great arsenal of the natural world where all his facts are stored, and, after passing them in review, to select those that he may bend most perfectly to his will, which he in turn has made subservient to the architectural scheme. To apparently annihilate compulsory limitations of area; to relieve the monotony of the regular and equal proportions that architecture, of necessity, imposes—these are among the problems with which the mural painter has to deal; and it is this exacting and intellectual demand that gives added dignity to the achievement, rendering such exercise of hand and brain worthy to be entitled *"le grand art."*

Another reason, which lies deeper than the prohibitory lack of exhibition space, has prevented our developing this noble art. It is one also that may not perhaps be so immediately remedied—viz., the want of general public instruction in the elements of drawing and painting. Primary schools in France give pupils an elementary acquaintance with art which creates a demand later on for some kind of graphic supplement to the legends and facts of history that they have absorbed at school. Then, too, local pride tends to foster the art instinct there as perhaps in no other country. A youth in any distant *département* or unimportant French town who shows peculiar aptitude for drawing and painting is often encouraged and aided by a public purse to continue the cultivation of his gifts in the art schools of Paris. As records of his progress there and in recognition of this assistance, he sends home from time to time examples of his work, which become the property of his native place. I was often surprised, when first living in France, to come across paintings of superior quality in the museums of comparatively insignificant towns, and it was only after a prolonged sojourn there that I learned the source of these unusual acquisitions. They proved to be oftentimes the productions of a local genius who, on the road to fame, had acknowledged municipal benefactions by perhaps a "success" from the Salon, or the customary contribution expected of him by the authorities. Might we not here in our own country follow some such course with profit?

It is no great matter of surprise, then, that we, as a people, have but recently awakened to the larger purposes of art. And many of these larger purposes are served through the medium of decorative painting. The sweep and requirements of decoration are boundless, its function wide and all-embracing; for its mission is to adorn the various activities of life with appropriate and harmonious illustration. Despite the drawbacks which have hitherto impeded our advancement in mural art, there is still for us, owing to the force of native talent, an encouraging outlook which heralds even brilliant results.

Perhaps in no other sphere of artistic effort is there so much demanded of the painter as in this very one of mural embellishment; and I sincerely believe that it is a branch which, if better understood, would be more generally regarded with the high respect that is due to it. In the first place, the pursuit of this art implies a life of subjection on the part of the painter; he works each moment trammelled by conditions that are not of his own making but of those who have gone before him, both architect and builder, leaving behind problems which he alone must confront. In addition to this, his exhaustive studies from nature must necessarily have been of wider range than those of specialists in art—the painter of figures only, or the portrait, marine, animal, or landscape painter. All these elements are likely to be called for in the execution of some interior design; and these must be made so subservient to the requirements of mural fitness that they become practically of another world in matter of color and a certain conventional synopsis of form. Then, too, in point of subject alone, scenes of fable, history, legend, or classic idyl biblical story or splendid epic, must find a sympathetic harbor in the mind of the painter who would acceptably fill the rôle of grand illuminator of the present and of the past.

The general prevalence of large fortunes has given us the right to expect that a portion of this treasure will be expended by its owners after the manner of enlightened possessors of wealth in Europe, viz., by calling on those whose taste and study have prepared them to beautify and embellish our dwellings; and not the home only, but all those places where humanity meet to carry on the functions of a civilized existence. First of all, let me mention a few that are now being thus ornamented: Sir Frederick Leighton is engaged in decorating an important panel of the interior of the Royal Exchange, London; while Bowdoin College, Maine, and the Boston Public Library have recently employed a number of our own artists to adorn their walls; and in the case of the latter institution the services, as well, of that veteran French mural painter, M. Puvis de Chavannes, have been secured to make a series of designs for the enrichment of the staircase. This is surely encouraging. But our museums, opera houses, music halls, not to speak of libraries, hospitals, and railway stations, are, with few exceptions, practically barren of mural ornamentation by professional painters.

These large opportunities are still open, nay, they are multiplying; but bequests to hospitals and universities will in time make them realizations in these institutions, and I expect to see even railway stations become a factor in disseminating a taste for the fine arts. Few places could be made more inviting to high effort on the part of the decorator than these utilitarian structures. Here the waiting passenger—the untried youth starting out to face the world, and the newly landed immigrant—might find something in these pictured panels to cheat the hour, stimulate ambition, or to encourage hope. Stations should be built to accommodate this work; and as a means of carrying art's message to the masses this method would be unsurpassed, thronged as these places are daily with hosts which scatter to the four quarters of the land. Our banks also might be appropriately decorated; for subjects suggesting the various business activities that create them, and from which they draw the "sinews of war," may be illustrated on their walls with much effect and pertinence. And where could themes from history, biography, the classics, be more fittingly delineated than on the walls of institutions of learning? Great events of the past should there be pictured by a master, and thus salient points of history impressed on the student's memory, while at the same time he would make a step in aesthetic culture. Portraits of great men, too, will not be out of place here—scientists, inventors, poets, writers of fiction, historians and statesmen looking down from their frames might become sources of inspiration and incentive to those who are preparing themselves for the various labors of the world.

The propriety of illuminating the walls of colleges and churches is so obvious that it will be enough to mention the fact here that these precincts in most civilized countries have been peculiarly favored in this matter, and I will cite only the Grand Opera House, Hotel de Ville, the Sorbonne and the Panthéon in Paris, as the more recent recipients of this distinction. During the past twenty years the interiors of these three buildings have in some instances received the crowning work of a painter's lifetime, notably in the case of Baudry at the Grand Opera House; and it is a significant fact that, with slight exceptions, the honor of such commissions has been awarded to men of acknowledged achievement and highest reputation in their art.

But the culmination of the decorative spirit will perhaps be reached only when the architect, the painter, and the sculptor work together from the inception of the structure to its completion. From the present condition of things this sounds like a dream—it may become a reality. Should a building be projected here in which the arts of architecture, painting, and sculpture might go hand in hand from start to finish, it may not be too much to say that it is well within the possibilities of the American temperament to set a model for the world. It is indisputable that such a course pursued by a people in any special department of intellectual effort tends to perpetuate a high standard of accomplishment in that particular field, and thus secure a present, and promise of future, excellence that holds them up to the admiration of mankind. This excellence we may make our own by intelligently improving our splendid opportunities. For, to briefly recapitulate, the multifarious occupations of a young and growing country will be used as suggestive themes reducible to lofty treatment by means of mural art. In this art, as I have already shown, business enterprise may be turned to aesthetic account, and transportation, freight-traffic, and agricultural pursuits become fit subjects for noble illustration. So, too, will scholarly research, religious life, the diversions of society, and all the amusements and recreations of mankind be brought to the service of an art that shall be as omnipresent as light itself, and in a certain sense as vivifying.

11. MUNICIPAL ART

CHARLES H. CAFFIN

Time and man together have made the cities of the Old World. Not infrequently man has been the builder, time the artist. In America, however, the rapidly expanding needs of the community have been constantly treading on the heels of time, and accelerating its pace at the expense of its dignity. Our cities, especially in the West, like Topsy, have "just growed," and with as little consciousness of cause and effect. First there has been sprawling, incoherent babyhood, in which everything is tolerated that makes for development; then the growth to hobbledehoy—big-framed, uncouth, obtrusive, but vigorous and full of promise; later, the period of youth, that begins to feel itself to be something and has glimmerings of pride in its personal appearance, displaying it particularly in an exaggerated taste for embellishments; still later, the manhood, with its sense of responsibility and acquired dignity of demeanor, its tendency

Harper's Monthly, 100 (April, 1900), 655–66.

to form alliances and to grow into its place in the community. By this time the individual pride has become broadened and fixed; it expresses itself in the personal surroundings of home, in the environment of business, and finally in the general dignity and beauty of the city. Individualism, without being swamped, has merged itself in the communal idea.

It is a stage of development corresponding to this last one that the American cities are entering upon to-day: the transition from individualism to civicism as the vital force. It goes without saying that the debt we owe to individualism is incalculable. It is the prevailing note in American character, the source of the nation's extraordinary development, and the foundation of our system of government. Yet there is no need to make a fetich of it. Unduly exercised, it may even put a check upon progress. We select the four horses of a team for individual qualities, certainly, but expect them to pull together for the purpose of moving forward the coach. There must be a controlling force on the box to see to it that individualism does not pull in opposite directions and stultify or impede itself. This same individualism, too, is not necessarily individuality. It is often a concentration on self rather than an expansion of self; and in selfish indifference to everything which does not concern its immediate interests, trades its birthright to a boss, and leaves to anybody or nobody the control of public issues. In both of these ways individualism has affected the appearance of our cities—positively by a rampant assertion of itself, and negatively by a disregard of its responsibilities to the community. Buildings are erected with reference to no other consideration but the personal interest of their promoters. Some of them are mere mushroom growths, intended to subserve only immediate necessities; others are built to remain, and with praiseworthy intention that they shall be impressive. But in each case their relation to other buildings and to something of a plan in the general character of the neighborhood has been entirely ignored. There has been no controlling influence, either of public sentiment or of official authority. The municipal governments have had their own axes to grind, and municipal art or the material dignity of the city has not been one of them. There has been no public opinion to stir them into action in the direction either of control or of initiation. They have left the individual to his own devices, and neglected their own duty of tackling the municipal problems. The result is heterogeneousness and confusion.

It is not that our cities are ugly—far from it—but that they present a higgledy-piggledy agglomeration of many styles, dimensions, and degrees of good, bad, and indifferent, with little method and no regard for harmony of effect. Have you ever watched the row of gas-lights in front of the proscenium of a theatre while the overture is being played? Now here, now there, they leap or spread or jag themselves in sympathy with the particular note in the music to which each corresponds in vibrations. Fix this row of flame forms, and you will get something of the indiscriminateness of the sky-line of, say, New York city. Both are the expression of a simple law of cause and effect, unpremeditated, unregulated, and irresponsible, and both in response to music. For, I take it, the great groundswell of human endeavor heaving in a big city has a music to it, if we have the ears to hear it, and just as surely does the city's architecture express it. As men are, so they build—unconsciously, perhaps, but inevitably; and while the individual building reveals the degree of elevation or sordidness in the motive of the man who built it, the aggregate of these buildings, the city itself, will express the average civilization of the community. Even the unimpressionable man feels the truth of this in foreign cities, but is blind to it at home. He is so much a part of his city, and so inextricably entangled in divers ways with other parts of it, that he finds it difficult to detach himself sufficiently to see it in its corporate entity. Yet no doubt he has a glimmering of it at times—for example, when he views New York from the harbor. Daily he passes back and forth on the ferry, too preoccupied to regard the city in any other light than as the place whither he is hurrying to business. Once in a while, however, he has a moment of intuitive vision. The water of the harbor, dancing in the sunlight, speaks to him of bright and buoyant movement; the vast expanse of blue sky, cloudless and penetrable, of aspiration. The huge buildings, from a distance composing into one, form a towering mass of human endeavor, from which a thousand steam wreaths curl and soar and vanish, as if the spirit of the city were still struggling higher. The scene is transfigured. It is no longer an outcome of real-estate transactions, of the stress and struggle of competing units striving to get bread or to grow rich, but an embodiment of the corporate life of the community, of its virtues and imperfections, its facts and its ideals, and in a fuller sense than usual he feels "it is good to be here." Or, returning earlier than his wont from work some winter's night, he gazes on the innumerable lights. They flit across the water in every direction, or climb up into the dark vault and hang like a constellation—low down to earth, yet soaring high enough to dwarf the watcher into infinitesimal minuteness. He knows that each light bespeaks a single cell in a vast hive of human effort, but it is the mass that for the moment kindles his imagination—this marvellous presentment of combined energies. He glories in being a part of it, and feels lifted out of his little self into a bigger and fuller purpose. He realizes the dignity of the civic life. It is detachment that has given the true perspective, while a closer inspection reveals much that is brutal, amorphous, incoherent. The one way of seeing discovers the soul of the matter; the other, its obvious imperfections.

What many minds are seeking to-day is how to lessen these imperfections, and to make the outward form of the city a more harmonious embodiment of its indwelling spirit. There is no need to apologize for stating the case this way, although to some it may seem transcendental. The soul of a city—why not? It is a convenient method of describing the composite impulses which are aggregated within its limits; and it is not until these are taken into account and their true significance recognized that a worthy civic pride is engendered. As soon as a number of citizens realize the relation between this net-work of appearances and the energizing force, soul, or what you please to call it, within them, they will not rest until the latter is embodied in a form that expresses it worthily. This was the impulse that made Venice, for example, so noble an embodiment of the genius of her inhabitants. No doubt the Italian instinct naturally feels after the artistic, and there was more homogeneity of population in Venice than in some of our cities, but otherwise the conditions were not dissimilar. Venice was a city of traders. Wealth and success "talked" then as they do now. But also there was the ambition that the talk should be enduring, and expressive in no uncertain way of the dignity of the civic life. Frankly it was ostentation; not of the individual, however, but of the community; and not of the community's sordid and vulgar characteristics, but of its worthiest and most beautiful. And how her artists caught the inspiration! There is but one St. Mark's in the world, for the simple reason that there is but one Venice; and all her boundless activities in the Orient, the ideals of her people, the very characteristics of her sky and water, are crystallized in this shrine, whose glories are the apotheosis of herself. True, the government was an oligarchy, and Venice was the creation of a few men in successive generations, while America is democratic, and the voice of the people is the power that counts. Here is the difference of the problem.

We have the same two forces to-day—the individual and the municipal; but the latter can no longer be the enlightened judgment of the few, but of the many—a widespread public opinion. To create it is the first important step towards beautification of our cities. If there is one thing more than another that we lack in our big communities and need, it is this same public opinion; not a prejudice in favor of this or that party, still less a prairie fire of excited sentiment kindled by the press to burn itself out, but a surely planted, steadily progressive popular conviction, based on civic pride, and acting along lines of expert control. This would be at once a check on excessive individualism and an incentive to municipal action. In some cities of Europe the check is exercised by the municipal authorities. As things are with us, that is not for the present to be expected or desired. The cultivated classes hold aloof from public affairs, and the politicians are concerned with the spoils. Already, under a pretence of control, the architect is thwarted in his plans, the contractor compelled to adopt certain methods and materials, in the interests not of the community but of its rulers. A thing "goes" to-day and is blocked to-morrow, just according to the amount of oil that lubricates the "machine." It is a mere conjecture how far even the conditions relating to health, safety of life and limb, and protection from fire are satisfied. To invite such a system to embrace control over artistic matters would be foolishness. The result would be worse muddle and corruption. I do not forget that in New York and Boston one of the departments of the city government is an art commission, and that Chicago contemplates a similar advance. But their powers are advisory, not initiatory. No work of art can be acquired by the city or set up in its public places without having been first approved by the commissioners; and the Mayor, at his discretion, is empowered to call upon them for advice in other matters. They are allowed no initiative, however, and there is nothing except public opinion to prevent the Mayor from ignoring their advice. Still, the mere creation of the art commission is an immense step forward. It is at least a legalized recognition that municipal government involves some questions of art. The wedge has been inserted, and it remains for public opinion to drive it home. At the risk of repetition, the main solution of the problem of municipal art rests in the establishment of this same public opinion. The voters in the last resort are the repositories of power. They are already a court of final appeal; they must form themselves into a body of initiative. Let us glance at what already has been done in this direction.

Municipal art societies exist in several cities. . . . [But] everything has been done under the immediate stimulus of public opinion in response to civic pride. There is a lesson in this. Taken in connection with the smaller results in other cities, it surely demonstrates that the main thing needed is public opinion; that the associations *per se* are of limited value unless they are backed by the same; and that what they need to do is to widen both the scope of their intentions and the number of their members. To repeat a previous simile, they are the thin end of the wedge, which must be driven home by the force of many. Assuming that these associations are necessary in their respective cities, they should be made the nucleus of an active propaganda. In every precinct a local branch should be formed, affiliated with the central society, but concerning itself immediately with the interests of its own district. This would involve much work, but surely there are already enough adherents of the cause to undertake it. The *modus operandi* might be somewhat as follows: The school authorities would no doubt permit the use of a room for the purposes of a meeting-place. It should also be possible to find six residents who would form themselves into a committee to start an interest in the matter, and bring together in public meeting a fairly representative gathering. The talk, which might be illustrated with the stereopticon, should be of a nature to arouse enthusiasm, but still so simple and practical that every listener could carry away some definite suggestion. The dignity and refreshment of the oak should be urged, but the main thing should be to distribute a few acorns, and to encourage the planting and nurturing of them. The speakers, therefore, would have to make a special study of the particular district, so as to be able to offer a few plain hints, no matter how simple—referring, for example, to the tidiness of the streets and sidewalks, ash-barrels, the blocking of the sidewalks, advertising signs, and so forth. A pride and interest in little things would soon grow to larger issues. To many minds this advice will be as little attractive as the suggestion to wash in Jordan was to Naaman. "If the prophet had bid thee do some great thing"—but these little beginnings, this gradual growth, how very uninspiring! Yet this is the natural law of growth. The reason we have so little public opinion is because the public conscience, judgment, taste, are only intermittently appealed to, and then with great upheavals and upon some burning issue, as of sound money or rotten politics. Self-absorption is aroused to momentary enthusiasm or annoyance, as the case may be, then settles back into itself, more case-hardened than ever. It is like trying to tone the system with a debauch.

In our zeal for a public opinion in matters of taste we must not imagine we are creating a new thing in American municipal life. It is very much of a revival. The old buildings, say of fifty years ago, which still survive bear witness to good taste. The residences reveal the gentle breeding of their builders. They are characterized by form and proportion; there was neither the opportunity nor the desire for much embellishment. But taste and gentle manners were demoralized by the phenomenal advance in wealth. It demanded display beyond the ability of the artists to satisfy it artistically, and the results were extravagant and meretricious. Now it is different. Wealth has obtained the leisure to be cultivated; a new generation of architects, sculptors, and painters has arisen, who have garnered the experience of the world, and skilled craftsmen abound. A new era of taste has begun, directed to larger problems, and with more adequate means of solving them.

A few of these problems may be noted, and first those which belong chiefly to the individual. Without attempting to exhaust the subject, one may look at the matter from the points of view of the capitalist, storekeeper, and resident.

The capitalist builds primarily for rents. He would not be fulfilling his use in the community if he did not. The more successful he is in securing rents, the greater, as a general rule, the improvement of the neighborhood. He attracts other capitalists and a better class of tenants, all of whom are interested in the proper care of the streets, in questions of sanitation and police. He has found that to get higher rents he must offer more external and internal attractions. If these are not in the best of taste, it is directly the architect who is to blame, and indirectly the public, whose ignorance invites sham, vulgarity, and mere display. But the capitalist has also grown to be influenced by another motive—pride in himself and in his city. There is a further stage, which he is only just beginning to reach when he realizes that his own interest as well as the city's would be better served by merging individualism in a general harmony of effect, by resorting to co-operation rather than competition. A Napoleon the Third, with his Baron Haussmann, could introduce uniformity, and thereby impressiveness, into certain parts of Paris by his simple *ipse dixit*. The equivalent of that in democratic America will be a pooling of interests—syndication in city architecture, as in other departments of life. It has already been adopted here and there in the apartment-house districts, with the result of a harmonious arrangement that has maintained a uniform high standard in the block, and so attracted and kept a better class of tenants.

The storekeeper's first aim, also, is to secure customers. The appearance of his store is one of his methods of advertisement. It reflects most accurately the degree of refinement in the public he expects to attract. If one needs any proof of the absence and need of improved public taste it will be furnished *ad nauseam* by visiting the second and third rate shopping districts on a bargain day. Behind the counters, weary attendants, anæmic from much standing in poisoned atmosphere; in front of them, a jostling, sweating, hectoring crowd of shoppers, eager to waste their money on fripperies or to get something below its legitimate value—marked down as the result of bankrupt lives, of traders who have been forced under by the pressure of this hideous competition, or of operatives whose lives and those of their wives and children are ruthlessly sacrificed to this craze for bargains. Nothing can remove this curse of modern so-called civilization but an improved public opinion, which will grow to be ashamed to take something for next to nothing, and will prefer well-made, well-designed goods to garish shoddy.

But even among the more dignified stores how much room for improvement exists in the way of artistic shop fronts and trade signs! The average idea of attracting notice is by the use of letters, especially of big letters, which would be all very well if the neighbors did not adopt as big or bigger ones. But they do, and the result is a gilded jangle of announcements which defeat their purpose as completely as if each man in a crowd should shout at the top of his voice. How much more effectual it would be if a storekeeper obtained from an artist some sign characteristic of his business, which, executed in metal, wood, or marble, would hang from or be set into the front of his shop, attracting immediate attention by its individuality and beauty, mentioned everywhere as his, and identified with him and his business! In foreign cities awnings also are made a means of individual assertion, and much is done with flowers and shrubs.

In this last way the resident in house or flat could help to beautify the city. Window-boxes, for example, cost little, can be treated in a great variety of charming ways, and are a source of delight to the children of the family.

To the larger problems which await official solution when public opinion has prepared the way for it a brief allusion must be made. Stated concisely, the duty of an ideal municipal government would be to preserve what is good and remedy what is bad or inadequate in the past, to regulate the present, and to have a prevision for the future; in fact, to maintain as far as possible the continuity of the city's life. We unhesitatingly approve the preservation of Independence Hall in Philadelphia, of Faneuil Hall and the façade of Bullfinch's State House in Boston, but in these and other cities there have been many landmarks of history irretrievably lost. Patriotic and historical societies have been instrumental in saving much, but in a proper condition of public opinion this would be one of the important cares of the municipal authorities. Every surviving landmark should bear a tablet, on which the younger generation may read its record, and when advance sweeps away the home of some great man or the scene of some great event, a suitable memorial, be it only an inscription upon the building which supersedes it, should perpetuate the memory.

But the remedying also of the past is one of the official problems. The early growth of our cities responded to present needs which could not anticipate the subsequent enormous development. . . .

Municipal control should be exercised in limiting the height of buildings, and in insisting that buildings henceforth erected upon narrow streets shall have the ground-floor fronts set back to permit of arcades. Public opinion, as it forms, will also demand that the focal points of the city—where, for example, several important streets intersect—shall be embellished with fountains or statuary, and that all fixtures, such as toilet-rooms, drinking-fountains, seats, light-standards, and newspaper-stalls, shall be artistic in character.

Lastly, with an eye to the future, the planting of trees in our streets will be encouraged, all franchises will be made a source of revenue, and in every public work undertaken provision will be made for later needs. It is a particularly creditable feature of the design for the New York Public Library that it contemplates an extension upon the west side, when needed.

IV

Architecture

The country's variety of climates and cultures prevented the dominance of a single architectural style. Earlier designers had used a "federal" or Gothic style for public buildings, but there was a great variety of styles in lesser buildings. A spare, utilitarian design rose naturally from new post-Civil War commercial needs, best exemplified in grain elevators, warehouses, train sheds, and machinery. But this simplicity was not "elevating" enough for many builders and patrons, who were still uncomfortable in the presence of undisguised power. They often cloaked the most sophisticated technology—electrical and heating systems, elevators, steel frames—with decorations to avoid the accusation of displaying mere material power.

The same divided thinking permeated home construction. Many new houses were carefully planned, with light and airy rooms segregated according to use. Housewives also adopted laborsaving conveniences. But many home exteriors revealed the owner's and designer's apparent need to cover utilitarianism with "uplifting" but unintegrated decoration. Yet at their best, these houses expressed individuality, and the love of color and variety.

Sharp debates within the emerging architectural profession added to the public's confusion. Architects wished to retain American qualities, while accepting an international style. They also hoped to control the development of individual buildings in cities, and to shape specially planned urban and suburban areas.

Though professionalism touched architecture, it was also an era of great individual talents. Henry Hobson Richardson developed a rich neo-Romanesque style that seemed to answer America's desire for the grand, without being grandiose. Louis Sullivan was among the first to create an integrated commercial style. And the firm of McKim, Mead, and White, best known for the Boston Public Library, worked in an elegant modified classicism suitable to formal public architecture.

The crosscurrents in architecture vividly illustrated the difficulties of meeting new demands with old formulas. Architecture also showed the impact of both an older European mannerism, and the sudden demands of new urban-commercial building.

12. THE DIFFICULTIES OF
MODERN ARCHITECTURE

A. D. F. HAMLIN

Modern civilization has very unequally affected the fine arts. While sculpture in its methods and principles remains essentially the same art as in the days of Phidias, painting has been revolutionized by the discovery of new media of expression and new fields for its exercise. Oil- and water-colors, the scientific treatment of perspective and of the principle of values, landscape-painting, and, to a certain extent, *genre* as well, are peculiarly

Architectural Record, 1 (October-December, 1891), 137–50.

modern developments of the pictorial art. But it is in architecture that the changes have been most radical and far-reaching. Standing midway between the fine and the useful arts, architecture partakes of the nature of both; it is the finest of the useful arts and the most useful of the fine arts. It is, therefore, alike subject to those influences which affect the expression of sentiment in plastic form, and to those which concern the practical life and needs of society. In that strongly artistic period of Italian art which we call the Cinque Cento, we find architecture chiefly occupied with pure beauty of form, increasingly devoted to the purposes of public and private rather than of religious life. As physical science advances and life becomes more complex on its material side, it is only natural that practical and utilitarian requirements should become more imperative, relegating purely artistic considerations ever further into the background. This is precisely what happened in the case of architecture, which is to-day a different art, not only from that of the antiquity or of the Middle Ages, but also and even from that of the early Renaissance. It is prosecuted under different conditions, with different materials and processes; it is controlled by different considerations, and is called upon to supply different requirements. Those who complain of the failure of modern architects to profit by those historic examples of their art which are the admiration of all men, ignore or forget how difficult of application are the principles these exemplify to the special conditions prevailing in modern work. Conceived in another age, for other uses, and under conditions long since vanished, they can serve as models for modern practice only in the same way in which the epics of Homer or of Dante have stood as models for the study of writers of all subsequent ages. The fundamental principles of composition, construction, design, proportion and ornament, these triumphs of the builder's art certainly illustrate in consummate fashion, and are therefore ever worthy objects of study and admiration. But to apply the lessons they teach to the wholly new conditions created by modern life is no easy problem. Conscientious and highly-gifted architects have long been devoting themselves to this problem with varying success. If their failures have been many and their triumphs few, as some would have us believe, it is at least conceivable that the difficulties of the problem, and not the incompetence of the architects, may be the cause; but upon the architects usually falls the blame. The responsibility for the failure of modern architecture to reach the high level of past attainment, it is not wholly easy to rightly apportion. Many of those who have in recent times written on this and similar topics have shown themselves as incapable of discrimination and judgment in estimating what modern architecture has done or is doing, as they are ignorant or insensible of the actual conditions, requirements and limitations which prevail in modern practice. For this reason they fail to touch the true causes of the shortcomings they deplore, and instead of contributing to their cure they rouse futile and acrimonious discussion, bestow sweeping and unmerited blame, and fill the public mind with mistaken notions and unfounded suspicions. It seems, therefore, high time to call attention to some of the real difficulties of the problem of modern architecture. Certain preliminary considerations will first be in order, which if trite, are nevertheless fundamental.

The first of these relates to the twofold nature of the art, to which allusion has already been made. Architecture has its origin in the material needs of mankind, and these must necessarily control its development. It has furthermore to deal with the stern laws of gravitation and of the strength of materials, to whose behests all its manifestations must be subordinated. In these aspects, then, it is purely utilitarian, and if it stops here, is not an art, but a science or a trade; it is mere building or engineering. It rises to the dignity and glory of an art only when it consults the demands of beauty and grace, seeking to reach the emotional side of man as well as to minister to his material wants. Mere fitness to an end is not artistic beauty, nor even an element in it. Convenient planning and stable, scientific construction may exist in—nay, they frequently seem to demand—forms and combinations wholly unpleasing to the eye. The demands of use and beauty not infrequently pull in opposite directions, as every architect knows. It is a sophism as hollow as it is common, that beauty consists mainly in fitness and appropriateness. It is time that this fallacy, based as it is on a truth, were exploded. "Beauty is skin deep" in the sense that it relates only to external and visible form and color, not to function and internal structure. A wholly beautiful building or design may prove entirely lacking in convenience and appropriateness. The two kinds of excellence—utilitarian and æsthetic— are independent of each other. It is, however, true that when they coexist in one design, so that the perfect structure serves at once the ends of use and of beauty, each enhances the other; and herein we find suggested the true purpose and function of architecture. It is *to harmonize in one and the same creation, the independent and oft-conflicting claims of use and beauty,* so that the very forms devised to meet practical needs in the most perfect manner shall also satisfy the human craving for beauty, grace, refinement. In the highest types of historic architecture the beauty we admire is inherent. It is a part of the building, an outcome of its whole plan and construction, which have been made to serve the ends of beauty at the same time that they meet the practical purposes for which the structure was designed. In engineering works, fitness, stability, and economy absolutely control the design, grace and beauty being sacrificed to these practical considerations; while, on the other hand, every design whose beauty is merely the adventitious grace of ornament, or in which beauty is produced only at the cost of convenience and sound construction, drops at once into the category of bad architecture, however excellent, viewed merely as a decorative composition.

It is beside our purpose to enter at present into the question of the modern use of styles, further than to call attention to the real meaning of the term. A style is nothing but the customary and characteristic system of construction and ornament prevailing in a given time and place. It is the outcome and product of all the social, political, economic, intellectual and artistic conditions that govern the age and people that practice it, and can change only as those conditions change; that is, in the same way with languages and literatures. No man, nor any set of men, can create a new style, nor has there ever been in history any sudden change in styles, except as the consequence of the overthrow of one civilization by another. Even the Renaissance in Italy brought no sudden revolution in architectural forms. It is surprising to see how far back into the Middle Ages the beginning of Renaissance architecture can be traced. Each so-called new style builds on what has gone before, in the near or remote past. As time goes on, erudition and archæology place at the architect's disposal increasingly rich mines of historic form, which it is his right and prerogative to draw upon freely. But with this greater range of choice comes the greater difficulty of choosing and combining, while a thousand influences beyond the architect's control operate to hamper the free expression of his own artistic imagination. The difficulty of rational and artistic design grows with the relaxation of established precedent, consequent upon this vast widening of the field of selection. The confusion of styles, that is, the mixture in one building, or the contemporaneous use in different buildings, of forms borrowed or imitated from distinct historic styles, thus finds its natural explanation in the intellectual spirit of the time, which in all branches tends to archæology and eclecticism. Whether this is or is not to be deplored, and what its present tendencies and final outcome may be, are questions by no means to be answered off-hand. They may be reserved for future consideration, as their discussion would too far transcend the limits of this article.

In the third place it should be considered that whoever would criticise modern architecture must carefully distinguish between shortcomings rightly chargeable to the architect, and those which exist in spite of him and constitute the conditions under which his work is done. This requires a practical acquaintance with the profession and its *personnel* which some earnest writers seem to lack. The critic must know what are and what are not representative modern works. He must separate tendencies that have "run out," and shortcomings that are fast disappearing, from those which are on the increase. He must distinguish between the creations of acknowledged leaders in the profession and the mass of commonplace work emanating from the nobodies who have neither taste nor training. It is of course possible to draw instructive lessons even from this lowest stratum of the builder's work, but these lessons do not pertain to architecture, and the failings they set forth should not be imputed to any one but the authors of such productions. The critic must also understand the relations of architect and client, and the limitations imposed by local conditions as to materials, space, expense, the demands of commerce and the degree of public education and culture in the community. It is the failure to make these and similar essential distinctions and to institute just comparisons that vitiates some of the most recent writing on modern architecture. . . .

Keeping in mind these considerations, let us see how they bear on the main question before us.

It becomes evident, in the first place, that just in proportion as material and utilitarian requirements become exacting will the architect find himself hampered in the artistic expression of his conceptions. The problem of harmonizing the demands of utility and taste must grow more and more difficult as the claims of material comfort and scientific construction become more numerous, complicated and unbending. But this is precisely the case with modern work, which must first of all meet the practical requirements of a life infinitely more complex than that of any preceding age. Science has created innumerable wants which the architect must satisfy, whatever else he may omit to do. Sanitary engineering demands a complicated and elaborate system of contrivances for the proper heating, ventilation and drainage of even the commonest private dwelling. Steam, gas and electricity must enter the service of the householder, traveling through countless pipes and insulated wires to furnish heat, light and power, to actuate bells and burglar-alarms, or to communicate thought. Gas engines and steam engines, pumps and elevators, ventilating fans and dumb-waiters, coal vaults and ice chests must be hidden away in the recesses of the construction, and yet be within the easiest access. Our modern social life requires its special arrangements of drawing, and reception, and dining, and music rooms; the private life of the family must be accommodated with its bedrooms and dressing-rooms, studies, libraries and sitting-rooms, its closets and bath-rooms, all arranged for the greatest comfort and convenience of the inmates as to access, retirement and inter-communication. Add to these elaborate requirements the stern limitations of the building laws and the restrictions imposed by the size and shape of building-lots in the larger cities of the modern world, and we find ourselves, even in the planning of a dwelling house, face to face with an exceedingly complex and difficult problem. For within these compact limits of size and shape the architect must meet every one of the multifarious conditions enumerated above and many others before he can even begin to think of artistic proportions and a lovely exterior. The client is inexorable in resisting any sacrifice of convenience or comfort to mere beauty, and he is quite right. Architecture is his servant, not his master, and it is the architect's duty to work beauty into the forms born of these hard conditions, not to attain it by disregarding the conditions. Undoubtedly the task is difficult. Let those who bewail the inferiority of modern to mediæval art consult the article "Maison" in Viollet-le-Duc's "Dictionnaire Raisonné," and they will realize the difference between the poor, comfortless mediæval house of two or three rooms within damp stone walls, with its narrow passages, tortuous stairs, and unsanitary arrangements, to which not even the French author's eloquence can make us blind—and the elaborate combination of rooms, halls, stairs, sliding-doors, baths, closets, kitchens and scientific contrivances which constitute the house of the average dweller in a modern city. He will perceive what few seem to realize—the immense difficulty of the modern problem of house-designing as compared with that of the period he so admires. Moreover the conditions change nowadays more in ten years than in a century of the Middle Ages, so that past experience is soon out of date and useless, whereas in olden times the slightest modifications sufficed to adapt the solutions of one decade to the problems of the next. What modern architects have accomplished within these untoward limitations offers at least as much to admire as to deplore. Especially in Modern American country houses of not excessive cost is there to be found a remarkable combination of careful, logical and artistic planning, in which comfort, health and convenience are admirably provided for, with charming and picturesque exteriors, inviting and full of character. In these houses there is doubtless much to criticise; but the faults are those of a nascent and virile art, still in process of development. If Pliny's delightful Laurentine villa was planned with reference solely to the varied exposures of the different wings and chambers to the sun, the shade, the sea, and the various prevailing breezes, the architect certainly deserves the credit of his success in meeting those requirements. But it is probable that any modern architect of reputation under the same social and economic conditions would have solved the problem at least as well, perhaps better. For the fact that modern clients, with modern habits of life, refuse to live in endless one-story buildings attended by a vast retinue of slaves, and prefer, even in country estates, houses of two or three stories, with hot and cold water, gas, furnaces or steam heat, double walls, glass windows and verandas; in which they can be served by two or three servants instead of a few hundred, society, not the architects, should be held responsible.

But if the modern house is an intricate structure compared with that of the Middle Ages, and, indeed, of any bygone age, the developments of modern business in large cities have given rise to a class of structures presenting vastly greater difficulties of design and construction. The problem they present to the architect is one of the most knotty and perplexing that can be conceived, and the practical requirements are more unyielding and more varied than in any other class of designs he has to prepare. Upon a plot of ground usually narrow and irregular in shape, hemmed in by lofty buildings, he must erect an edifice many stories high, and divide it into the greatest possible number of offices, so arranged as to bring in the largest possible revenue. He is usually enjoined against "wasting" in courts and areas a foot of space not "absolutely necessary"—the proprietor usually constituting himself the judge of the amount required; while at the same time he is expected to provide all the offices with sufficient daylight. Everything being determined upon a basis of possible revenue, stairs and halls must be reduced as much, and partitions made as thin, as safety or the building laws will allow. The structure thus planned must be threaded and honey-combed with pipes and shafts, flues and chimneys; innumerable wires must be concealed in its walls and ceilings; and its basement be filled with machinery of various sorts. Every one of these things the architect must himself think out, provide for and specify in detail, whether or not he bestows attention upon the artistic possibilities of the building. He is likely to be far more severely blamed for a misplaced bell-button, or an inconvenient elevator, or for dark offices which the restrictions imposed by the proprietor alone have made inevitable, than for ill-studied and inartistic treatment of the architectural forms. In other words, material and practical requirements are by the conditions of the times made to wholly overshadow æsthetic considerations.

Modern processes of building, moreover, as exemplified in these monstrous many-windowed stacks of offices, still further hamper the free expression of artistic ideas. Iron and steel now form a large part of the framework of every important building, and the development of constructive forms in metal has naturally proceeded along the lines of engineering rather than of high art. In the Middle Ages engineering and architecture were practically one, both alike receiving their highest development in religious architecture, whereas modern engineering has busied itself mostly with railroads, bridges and factories, and similar utilitarian problems, to the suppression of any artistic development. Metal construction has followed in its lead, and the architect has to deal with the forms and processes which the market offers alike to the engineer and to him. It is only in rare instances that he is permitted to use these materials in the special shape and manner which his artistic taste would lead him to devise. Furthermore, new materials, building methods and appliances are constantly being invented, all of which the architect must appropriate and use to the best advantage if he would keep up with the times. The building thus becomes a truly mighty problem in construction, requiring an immense amount of scientific and practical knowledge of the most varied kind, and the constant application of elaborate mathematical calculations and geometric processes. It is safe to say that the designing of a great building like the Auditorium at Chicago involves problems of construction fully as serious and difficult as were ever encountered in the most stupendous of mediæval cathedrals. And in judging the results two facts must be remembered which reflect the highest credit upon the talent of modern designers. The first is that while the erection of a cathedral occupied usually from fifty years to three centuries, during all of which time the constructive problems it involved were being studied in the light of the experience acquired in other and similar buildings, it is not infrequently the case that a building like the Auditorium in Chicago, or the *World* office in New York, is completed and occupied within eighteen months or two years from the first inception of the plans. The second fact is still more significant, but rarely taken into consideration by the critics. During nearly the whole of the period from 1060 to (say) 1450—nearly four hundred years—architecture in all northwestern Europe was predominantly occupied with a single problem—that of cathedral design. In England, France, Germany, Spain and the Low Countries, and to a certain extent in Italy, the requirements of the cathedral or abbey church as to plan, arrangement and general construction were practically the same. In all these countries the one great preoccupation was to vault the nave and side aisles of the type-plan bequeathed by the early Christian basilica, and to execute these vaults in stone and in such a way as to provide a lofty clerestory and immense windows, with the minimum obstruction of the floor space by piers and columns. Gothic architecture received its whole character from this problem, and it required three hundred years at least of the combined efforts of ecclesiastic and monastic architects, assisted by the skill of the powerful bands of "lay builders" to reach such a consummate result as we admire in Amiens, Strasburg, York, Burgos or Antwerp. In our times no two successive problems present conditions or requirements as similar as are almost any two mediæval cathedrals of the same period; the experience of a quarter of a century ago is useless in dealing with the design of to-day; and the modern architect, instead of being able to devote a lifetime to one or two buildings as his contribution to the solution of a problem on which the whole confraternity of architects have been unitedly laboring for a couple of centuries, must in the course of a year or two solve twenty wholly diverse problems, not consecutively, but a large number at once, among which may be one or two quite as complicated as the designing of a mediæval abbey church.

The commercialism of modern life, which hedges in the architect with its inexorable demands, and measures his work not by its intrinsic merit but by its income-producing value, is furthermore curiously allied with a love of splendor and luxury which disregards expense. This usually takes the direction of personal comfort or of excessive display, seldom consistent with the most refined taste, but demanding what is showy and costly rather than what is really beautiful. This love of splendor the architect has to count with and minister to; he is thus compelled to prosecute his work under conditions adverse to any free expansion of his artistic nature. He is expected to master branches of knowledge the most diverse; he is compelled to consider requirements innumerable and harassing; he is constantly confronted with sordid considerations of cost and interest; he is held responsible for the proper expenditure of millions of money, and for the correct execution of the minutest details of the most extensive and complex structures. Dealings with contractors and sub-contractors by the score; the selection of plumbing appliances and gas fixtures; pesterings of stupid, self-conceited and unreasoning clients, who set up their own crude conceptions and vulgar taste against the cultivated taste of the architect; the adjudication of disputes between clients and builders, calculations of girders and trusses, thrusts and weights— these are cares and duties which try the capacity and patience of the modern architect wholly outside of the main task of designing the building and preparing the drawings for its erection. Amid such an untoward environment, and occupied with such perplexing cases, he is asked to solve problems of whose difficulty what has been already said can give no adequate conception. What wonder if the artistic faculties are warped and stifled; if considerations of the good and the beautiful seem less and less imperative; if his failures are many and his successes few in the task of reconciling his artistic inspirations with the heterogeneous and iron-clad demands of modern life and business, and the unformed taste, or bad taste, of a philistine *clientèle?* To reach the ideal solution of the problem, to extract from these hampering conditions results inherently beautiful, demands true genius, and the world has never been prolific of geniuses.

When one considers the results achieved in the domain of modern domestic architecture, to which brief allusion has already been made, one must recognize the existence of a vast amount of highly meritorious work, in which artistic beauty is admirably blended with practical excellence and scientific construction. In the architecture of modern commercial buildings, the failures are certainly more obvious, but the triumphs are numerous and praiseworthy. When we consider the immense difficulties of this branch of architecture, we cannot fail to be impressed with the talent and skill often brought to bear upon the problem. Even when the artistic aspect of these buildings is unsatisfactory—let us cite as an example the New York *World* building—one is compelled to admire the sound and often ingenious construction, the masterly dealing with extraordinary difficulties of planning and arrangement, and the taste shown in the details, while many of the most obvious defects prove on investigation to be due to the interference of a client in matters of taste, or the force of circumstances which the architect could not possibly control.

In the domain of public architecture, including theatres and halls of assembly and governmental buildings, the difficulties are of a different kind, and the opportunities for artistic expression greater than in commercial structures. The defects in such buildings are, however, greatest on the artistic side, in our own country at least, and for this our architects are certainly in a measure to blame. But here again we are met by the presence of the adverse environment amid which modern architects pursue their vocation. The universal commercialism, the constant pressure of utilitarian considerations, the lack of sympathy or appreciation on the part of clients and corporations for what is truly noble and lovely in art, the constant dinning of the question of cost, economy demanded precisely where liberal expenditure should be applied, and display called for where a sober economy were far better—all these influences tend to stifle the artistic spirit, and to reduce architecture as nearly as possible to the condition of a branch of engineering. In this department, moreover, as well as in religious architecture, the constant change in the requirements of buildings of the same class operates precisely as in domestic and commercial architecture to prevent any such continuous approach to a final and perfect solution as we find in earlier ages—in the Doric temples of Greece, for example; or in the Thermæ of Imperial Rome, or the churches of Mediæval Europe.

If these observations have assisted any reader to an appreciation, however imperfect, of the great difficulties which beset the development of modern architecture, he will perhaps view its shortcomings with greater lenience and its achievements with greater respect. An intimate acquaintance with the great body of its practitioners, not merely with the conspicuous leaders, but with many also of humbler reputation who pursue their labors modestly and faithfully in obscure places, would certainly lead to a high estimate of the general earnestness, conscientiousness and intelligence with which they endeavor to meet and solve the problems and overcome the obstacles they encounter. The proportion of highly-educated and thoroughly-trained men among them is increasing; architectural schools are multiplying, and amid all the confusion of styles which arouses the ire of the critics there is manifest a growing dignity and refinement in composition and detail. The future cannot be predicted, but it certainly is not without signs of promise. We are now in a period of transition, and suffer from all the difficulties inherent in such a period. Neither indiscriminate praise nor sweeping condemnation on the part of the public will help the cause of noble art at such a critical point in its development. It is to be hoped that the public, to whom the architect looks for his employment and his reward, may come in time to such an acquaintance with the nature of his work and with his own disposition and aims that the praise of the whole community shall be unstintingly awarded to every sincere and intelligent effort of his towards a pure and noble result, and its condemnation visit with merited severity all that is base and unworthy in this greatest of the arts.

13. THE PROFESSION OF ARCHITECTURE

J. P. COUGHLAN

It was only at some indeterminate time in recent years that the adjective "liberal" came to be generally accepted in America as applicable to the profession of the architect. Previous to that time, the country carpenter or stone mason, and the city jerry-builder or contractor, unhesitatingly made, as they still make, the most ancient of all professions do duty as a second string to their more commonplace vocations. Nowadays all that is changed. The demand for palatial and elaborate mansions, beautiful and commanding public buildings, and business structures that are epitomized cities in themselves, has gained for the architect a recognition of his proper position. The American Institute of Architects and the Architectural League have contributed to this result. Membership in either of these societies does for the architect what the diploma of a leading college does for the doctor or the call to the bar does for the lawyer.

The architect has even greater advantages than either the lawyer or the doctor in that he is in immediate touch with the two great interests of life, the industrial and the artistic. He works hand in hand alike with the sculptor and the painter, and with the great leaders of business enterprise.

THE EARNINGS OF AN ARCHITECT

The rewards of architecture, in America at least, are sufficient for any reasonable ambition. It offers a field and a fortune unequaled in any other profession. The man who builds up a large practice, either through his own ability or through influence and friends, commands a generous and certain income, and one that is rarely curtailed by "bad debts." As in all professions, there are great extremes, and the rewards depend entirely upon the man, his opportunities and circumstances. Many full fledged architects earn only fifteen hundred dollars a year, while

Munsey's Magazine, 25 (September, 1901), 837–40.

a few have incomes of a hundred thousand dollars. Among the ten thousand practising architects in the United States, there are a few favored ones who make a net income of more than the larger figure, but they are so exceptional as to be almost a negligible quantity.

In considering the earnings of the architect, there are two classes to be taken into consideration—the wage earner, and the man in business for himself. The latter's income comes entirely from his commissions. The former is a salaried employee, usually known as a draftsman until such time as he can blossom out for himself with the more glorified term engraved on a brass plate. Almost every architect goes through this preliminary stage.

The largest office in New York has a staff of about a hundred draftsmen, each one a competent architect, well grounded in all that pertains to his profession. The salaries paid to them range from eighteen hundred to five thousand dollars a year, the average being twenty five hundred dollars. Many are content with this comfortable certainty, and would rather hold to it than go out into uncertain waters at the helm of their own ship of business. Some add to their incomes by executing minor commissions in their own time, and now and then one will open an experimental office of his own, while still working for another.

In order to consider architecture as an investment, it is necessary to glance at the work of preparation and its cost. Some architects who have grown up in the profession have attended no institution, but none, so far as I have been able to learn, has gained a high place who has not devoted years to technical and practical study.

THE TRAINING OF AN ARCHITECT

"Before entering upon the study of architecture," says an authority on the subject, "the pupil should be a good writer and a fair arithmetician; that is to say, he should have a knowledge of decimals, fractions, square and cube root, and mensuration. He should be able to deal with simple equations in algebra, should have mastered the first three books of Euclid, and should possess a knowledge of practical plane and solid geometry. To these should be added free hand drawing, elementary physics, practical mechanics, and elementary chemistry."

There are now in America several universities having departments of architecture. The principal of these are the Massachusetts Institute of Technology, in Boston; Cornell, Columbia, and the University of Pennsylvania. In all these a four year course of architecture is given, and at its end the graduate is competent to become a junior draftsman in an architect's office, where he will learn the practice of his profession. And a vast deal he must acquire. He must be able to claim a good working acquaintance with the mechanical trades, the arts of the mason, carpenter, plumber, plasterer, tinsmith, blacksmith, painter, glazier, and decorator, not to speak of the sculptor and carver. After that he will have to acquaint himself with the principles of engineering and mechanics, statics, strength of materials, the theory of arches, beams, and columns, the flow of air and water, ventilation and drainage, and all the mathematics that attend the quantitative treatment of things. Then, too, he must be familiar with business matters, contracts, estimates, specifications, inspection of work, settling of accounts, adjustment of responsibility.

Moreover, all these would be of little use without capacity and attainment in art. The architect must have an inherent good taste, and with it the artistic skill and ability to produce artistic work. He must possess the knowledge that distinguishes the connoisseur, carried to the point of a technical acquaintance with historical precedents and the shibboleths of styles. So it is a mighty task that the youth has before him.

In order that his education may be complete, it is considered necessary for him to go abroad. The School of Fine Arts in Paris attracts students from all over the world. None of the American schools pretends to give more than a thorough grounding in the principles of architecture. Sometimes the student is urged to pass a year or two in an office before he goes abroad. A young architect of my acquaintance put it this way:

"After leaving Columbia, I had enough money to pay for my course in France, but only just enough, and I did not want to waste it. For that reason I took service in an architect's office here for a year or two, in order to discover what it was I wanted most to learn in Paris. You see, I could only afford to go there once, and I wanted to have the knowledge to take advantage of what they had to teach me."

While American students flock to the Beaux Arts, few are able to pass the severe examination, and the rejected ones seek the ateliers of distinguished sculptors, or travel. As a matter of fact, to the student who is not prepared to spend at least four years at the Beaux Arts, admission there is of little advantage, for only in the fourth year is he taught what he most wants to know, the preceding years being taken up with mathematics that could be acquired as well in America. But that fourth year is undoubtedly of great advantage.

TWELVE YEARS OF STUDY AND WORK

It is impossible to lay down hard and fast rules regarding the cost in time and money, of preparation for any of the liberal professions. Generally the future architect must pass at least twelve years, of which eight are spent in school and four devoted to practical work in an office, before he can claim to be really competent. The entire time may be passed in an office, but the youth will not advance so rapidly in the end as he would if he had gone to a technical school. As a student, he is expending from five hundred dollars a year upward. I do not think the average for eight years can be less than a thousand dollars a year. For his first two years in an office he may get a nominal stipend. At the end of ten years of study and work he should be able to command a fairly good salary, but at least two, and very likely four, more years will pass before he can be called a master of his profession. By that time he may have risen from thirty dollars a week to twice or thrice as much; in a few large offices the most responsible men draw a hundred dollars weekly, or perhaps even more. He starts out for himself whenever his courage inspires him to do so.

The architect proper, since I suppose we can only accord the full honors of the profession to the independent practitioner of it, is paid according to a fixed rate of five per cent on the total cost of the construction of the building for which he makes designs, and ten per cent upon interior decoration, furnishing, and sculptural adornment. The etiquette of the profession is rigid in enforcing that rate. Thus, it is easy to calculate that the architect who designs a million dollar office building receives a fee of fifty thousand dollars for his services.

This is by no means all clear profit. Only the architect in command of a big staff of draftsmen and clerks can expect these lordly commissions. Almost invariably time is a very important consideration; when a design for a big building is required, it is wanted as speedily as possible, that valuable land may not be left idle. The designing of such a structure may take from six weeks to a year, according to the architect's facilities for turning it out. Naturally, a firm that can put twenty or thirty men at work on the design is most likely to get the commission. Thus, while the large firms get the best and most profitable commissions, their expenses are enormous.

Like all professional men, the architect is reticent about his monetary rewards. But while a statement of a successful practitioner's earnings must be more or less a matter of conjecture, there are facts on which it can be based.

How Great Fees Are Earned

The architect of a new office building at the corner of Broad Street and Exchange Place, in New York, will have received one of the largest fees paid in the profession when his work is completed. The cost of the building is estimated at six million dollars; and, not counting the increased percentage paid for the designing of the sculptural ornamentation and interior decoration, the designer's charge will not be less than three hundred thousand dollars. Even though he has to pay an army of assistants out of this, his personal profit must be very large.

The architect of the new Hall of Records received a hundred and fifty thousand dollars. Twenty five thousand dollars is paid for the designing of each of New York's new school houses. Fees running into the hundreds of thousands of dollars have become tolerably common in all the chief cities of the country since the introduction of the skyscraper and the development of the costly modern dwelling.

It is wise to consider what the architect does for these fees. Of course it is understood that he prepares plans and working drawings, and superintends the construction, which seems simple enough; but the designing of the most unpretentious country house will occupy a single draftsman from five days to two weeks, while one that might not attract any special attention will represent the labor of two or three months. It would require years for one man to complete the plans for a modern city house like that of the late Cornelius Vanderbilt.

The designer's work does not begin with preparing a plan and supervising the building. And his chief concern is not to devise schemes of ideal excellence. He must design the best house possible to meet certain conditions of cost, space, situation, utility, and a hundred other things. He must first obtain full information about the kind of building required, whether the site is rocky—this has a bearing on the cost of the cellars— whether it is on a slope, what kind of water supply is to be provided for, the exposure to the sun, and the prevailing winds. He must consider the possibilities of drainage, and the attitude of the house to the surrounding scenery.

All this, bear in mind, is for a simple country house; in the city the architect has to surmount many engineering difficulties as well as architectural problems. Indeed, one prominent architect characterized his own work in designing the tallest skyscraper now in New York as an engineering feat, with architecture almost wholly eliminated. He compared the result of his work to a vertical steel bridge, with railroads running up and down inside it.

THE EXPENSES OF AN ARCHITECT

It will be seen, therefore, that if the income of an architect is large, his expenditure in money, time, and talent is also great. His income really represents what the merchant calls his "turn over," and in the percentage of profit which his "turn over" yields him must he find the reward of his own labor and investment.

The equipment of an architect's office is a matter of many dollars. For instance, it must have, if not a library, at least the nucleus of a library. A good architectural library can be begun on about two thousand dollars. When ten thousand dollars is expended, the average architect shudders to think of the cost of completing it. Architectural books are expensive, and, owing to the plates, they require delicate handling. Then, the office must subscribe to the professional papers if it would keep abreast of current affairs; and as architecture has no country, or rather is shared by all countries, the periodicals of many nations are almost a necessity. Instruments, office rent, and salaries swallow up a large amount annually.

There is another unavoidable and persistent drain on the architect's profits, resulting from the custom of selecting a design from general plans submitted by a limited number of competing architects, usually not more than three, chosen from among the members of the Architectural League or the American Institute of Architects. Of course the successful competitor receives a commission at the regular rate. The other two get a nominal compensation for their designs, but such payment rarely covers more than a small part of the outlay in having the designs prepared.

THE STANDING OF THE PROFESSION

The rewards of an architect are not all pecuniary. His has been called the greatest of all professions in that it is the most comprehensive. His position today is higher than it has ever been before, and he and his confrères are actuated by a loftier spirit than ever before. The members of the two societies already mentioned, which include all the notable designers in the country, are striving earnestly to place their calling in an unassailable position, and to secure full recognition of its commanding influence in art. That they are devoting their energies to the artistic development of their work speaks well for the future of the profession, and though we are laboring under the nightmare of the skyscraper at present, we are at last emerging from the vain and groping stage into a realization of the national importance of the art of fine building.

The establishment of the American Academy at Rome, practically by the private munificence of a few architects and artists, is one of the healthy signs among the recent developments of architecture. This excellent institution furnishes three years' training abroad, under the most favorable conditions, to a limited number of young architects and artists chosen by competition. The idea is not so much to regard the personal advantage to the individual student, but rather to consider the training of his talents as a benefit to his country. When we compare the few students at Rome with the number of architects now practising, it would seem that the effort was puny and trivial; but, after all, the architect is an artist, and should even one student out of the three that the academy aims to "finish" in three years fulfil the expectations formed of him, it would have an uplifting effect upon the artistic architecture of the nation.

14. AN "AMERICAN STYLE" OF ARCHITECTURE

BARR FERREE

With us, one of the most popular of modern architectural ideas is that there will some day be devised a truly original American style. Seldom has the popular mind made a greater error, or so openly expressed its ignorance of what Architecture really is, and of the conditions under which it is evolved. Architecture is not an article of manufacture that can be produced on demand. It is one of the things not affected by "supply and demand." We produce buildings, it is true, but few of our most pretentious attempts can be viewed with favor by the advocate of the "American style."

The study of the history of Architecture shows in the most positive manner that the great historical styles—which it is

Architectural Record, 1 (July-September, 1891), 39–45.

fondly hoped the American will surpass—are the products of natural evolution spread over centuries of time; and are the resultants of the action of very many causes. In one sense their existence is as natural as that of a plant or of an animal. Many attempts have been made to deliberately design an American style of architecture by devising certain ornamental details without undertaking to introduce a principle distinctively American. All, however, rest on the error of supposing that a style of Architecture is something that can be designed or drawn to order on a sheet of paper, much as a client would order his architect to prepare a drawing for a house in some special style. No architectural style originated in such a hypothetical fashion in the past, and amazing as is the fertility of American invention, there is no reason to suppose it can overcome the operation of a law of nature by such a method.

Architectural styles follow national boundaries very closely. National or ethnographic qualities are among the most important phenomena that have influenced their development. As a nation we are totally without the ethnographic unity which is essential to the production of an original art. A people composed of English, French, Germans, Italians, Spaniards, Russians, Austrians, Hungarians, Danes, Swedes, Norwegians, Poles, Turks, Armenians, Portuguese, Greeks, black, white and Mongol, Christians, heathen, infidel, cannot assimilate such diverse elements without many years of intermixture and solidification. We have ideas that are representatively American; we have American customs and methods, none of which can be mistaken for anything else, but we have not that quality which will give us an architecture of our own.

Then again, were there no ethnographic conditions; if the history of art did not expressly declare it to be something that cannot be made to order as a coat or a pair of trousers, our geographical and climatic conditions would render it impossible. Our country embraces a larger area than that occupied by any other civilized people under a single government. The British Empire is a confederacy in which each colony is permitted a large measure of political freedom without reference to the mother country; a great part of the Russian Empire is inhabited

by semi-barbaric tribes, leaving us quite alone with the largest
territory, for which it is proposed to devise a typical form of
building. No proposition could be more absurd.

Our land is of such extent, it covers so many degrees of lati-
tude and longitude that it would be impossible to impress any
one style of architecture upon it, except by law or the arbitrary
caprice of fashion. An architecture which would be suited to
the semi-tropical climate of Florida would be totally out of place
in the cold, bleak temperature of Maine. The salubrious climate
of California requires a very different kind of dwelling from that
adapted to the hot summers and cold winters of Pennsylvania
and New York. But difference in temperature alone is not the
only natural argument against the much-longed-for American
style. Rainfall, the diversity of our products, the wealth of our
resources, the very elements of our greatness themselves are
sufficient reasons why we cannot have a national style of
Architecture.

For, if we could, what section, what temperature, what
climate, what products shall be taken as thoroughly and representatively national? Shall the East or the West, the North or
the South claim the priority, and impose customs and methods
on regions to which they are unsuited? Shall we take an average
section without especially marked natural features, such as sur-
rounds New York, or shall we select some remarkable and note-
worthy district as California and the Yellowstone National Park
as the typical American region? Carried to its logical conclusion,
the selection of any one of these would end in a catastrophe
scarcely less momentous than that which convulsed the nation
on the slavery question. People in the South would find it impossible to live comfortably in a dwelling built for the North, and
the man of Maine and the man of Texas would forget their difference on the tariff in endeavoring to make themselves comfortable in houses that bore no relation to the climatic conditions
of their respective homes. The question is not one of the local
pride, of the prevalency of wealth or of culture, but purely a
matter of climate. It would be quite as sensible to insist that
every man, woman or child in the United States should wear

the same kind and amount of clothing, of the same material and make, as to argue for a national architecture.

The geographical limitations of Architecture form a very interesting study. All the great styles originated in comparatively small states, and among people who inhabited a country of fairly uniform nature. The concentration of energy caused by the confining of intellectual growth to the relatively small areas of the old world was a powerful factor in the evolution of architectural styles. It may not be altogether true that the smaller the area the more developed the architecture, but it is somewhat significant that the most perfect of all styles was produced in Greece, one of the smallest of countries, and in Athens, one of the smallest of Greek states. People have fewer things to think about in a small country than in a large one, and objects directly under their observation acquire a relatively greater importance through the want of variety of ideas and occupations.

With us it is very different. Our vast territory, our multifarious products, our mixture of races and nationalities, our diverse interests, our varied climate and our inexhaustible resources render it altogether impossible for us to hope to evolve a genuine and national style of Architecture, even if the question were one that admitted of deliberate evolution or could be seriously and carefully considered. The blending power of time and the absorption into one family of the many people who now form our nation may possibly do something towards bringing about the realization of the popular dream, but at so remote a period as not to be worth taking into account. In this age of active inventive resource and discovery no prophet is more discredited than he who announces that such and such a thing cannot possibly be done, but the conditions under which architectural styles have been developed in the past are so obvious and definite that were it not for some unfortunate attempts to accomplish the impossible, it would seem incredible that sensible people should sit down before a drawing-board to produce a new, original, genuine, and withal American style of architecture by means of a compass and a T-square.

Though the American architect may not devise a style that shall be exclusively his own and bring him enduring and world-wide fame, he is not reduced to blindly copying buildings of past time, nor has he cause to be dissatisfied with the methods under which they were evolved. A system of architectural growth which produced the great temples of Egypt, the palaces of Assyria, the sanctuaries of Greece, the vast baths of the Romans, the dome of St. Sophia, the rich rugged beauty of the western basilicas, the sturdiness of the Romanesque, the unparalleled grandeur of the Gothic cathedrals and the innumerable ramifications of Gothic art, and the sometimes debased forms of the Renaissance, cannot be looked upon as a method that is old-fashioned and out of date, useless or forgotten, antique or incompatible with modern ideas. Not all previous architecture is worthy of being copied, but that of it which is possesses such surpassing qualities of greatness and truth that no modern architect need be ashamed to use them as models. If he produces anything half so honest and good he will be doing well.

But it is quite unnecessary that the modern architect should resolve himself into a copying machine with no more individuality than a hektograph. It is as great an error to suppose that because we cannot have an American style we must unquestionably follow other people, as it is to search for this style. The great problem before the American architect is to mould architectural ideas and forms to the varied conditions of our national life and situation, and thus while not obtaining an architecture that may be American in outward aspect, will be American in purport and through adoption. He will not insist on the selection of one style and one plan for the whole of our vast area and our wonderfully diversified climate, but he will permit each section to solve its own problem in its own way. These conditions are of course indefinite, but not more so than the problem itself.

Throughout history the human mind exhibits points of similarity of startling distinctness; the longing for the unobtainable is one of the most persistent characteristics of the race. This feeling has undoubtedly at times brought about the invention of many desirable things, but it is not always the sensible and the useful that humanity craves. In the Middle Ages the philosopher's stone, which should turn all things into gold, was at once the most popular and absurd of superstitions. When the history of ideas in this country in the nineteenth century shall be written, the invention of an "American style" of Architecture will be pointed out as an illustration of the same delusion which animated people in the Middle Ages concerning the philosopher's stone. And just as we moralize on the nonsense of the gold-converting substance, so will future artists wonder that sensible, educated, wide-awake people should have imagined they could produce a style of Architecture by deliberately drawing it. It is not flattering to our good sense that we should be so thought of, but it is not more comfortable to see the making of styles attempted under our eyes and encouraged and applauded by those who should know better.

V

Music

American audiences had long supported choral music, variety shows, and liked the operettas of Offenbach and of Gilbert and Sullivan. Throughout the century, they hosted the world's famous singers. Rapid and inexpensive rail transportation permitted stars and companies to travel widely, while urbanization and affluence enlarged audiences. Teaching academies expanded the art-public's interest in both the performance and production of fine music. New printing techniques placed sheet music within the reach of many families, who also bought instruments. Millions of children regretted the growing adult interest in musical study, but the home "musicale" as well as the night at the opera became institutions.

This general interest focused in support for permanent orchestras and opera companies, and for adequate concert halls in the major cities. Intercity rivalry, as between Chicago and New York, and Boston and New York, also enhanced support for musical institutions. A body of critics emerged to analyze music, and to guide listeners.

The compositions of Edward MacDowell (1861–1908) won

a large audience and typified the search for an American style
in music. "Local color" in music was not confined to the United
States, and had vigorous practitioners in Norway (Grieg), Central Europe (Smetana and Dvorak), and in a Russian school.
This nationalistic trend revealed a growing concern to retain
individual typology in a world culture. The works of "mod-
erns" like Wagner and Richard Strauss also showed that the
general European tradition was still viable, and occasioned many
musical debates.

Opera posed some special problems to Americans. It seemed
aristocratic, and a people attached to realism did not easily
suspend disbelief in the opera house. Intrinsically more expensive to produce than symphonic music, a full operatic repertoire
was a luxury few but the richest cities could sustain. But it was
a golden age of performance, as every major European singer
and native talents toured the country. The names of a few
divas, such as Nellie Melba, entered the popular vocabulary,
as that of Jenny Lind had done a generation earlier.

America did not develop a national school of music, but
sustained a great variety of performance. Perhaps music more
than any other art form impressed on Americans the richness
of European culture, and indicated to reflective listeners how
subtly they had entered the mainstream of world taste.

15. THE ISOLATION OF MUSIC

WALDO S. PRATT

In looking back over the history of music as a factor in
modern culture one cannot avoid noticing at many points its
apparent separateness from other factors. Instances can often
be found where musicians have deliberately emphasized this

The Forum, 21 (June, 1896), 501–12.

isolation, making their art an esoteric mystery, to be fully made known only in the secret circles of the initiated. Wherever any line of human effort is elaborately followed as a technical specialty, as it must be by those who achieve the greatest progress in it, the tendency to an isolating conception of it is inevitable. The extremely rapid development of music in the last two centuries is due to the large amount of this specialistic pursuit of it, and the whole popular notion of music has naturally been much affected by this fact.

In saying this it is not forgotten that music constantly shows an intrinsic readiness to escape from academic and other arbitrary isolations. Its primitive forms seem to be all of a diffuse and popular kind. It is found to have flourished in all periods and countries. It has been warmly loved by millions of men, and has been passionately followed as a profession by thousands, representing the most diverse classes of society. It has now, after some strange vicissitudes, pushed its way into a remarkable prominence in what is called cultivated society. In spite of these facts, however, it has been common for musicians and others either to set music wholly apart from other agencies of culture, or so to minimize its influence that it may be disregarded in any serious and important summary. This disdain of music as a historic fact and a persistent social force is too often merely a part of a sweeping disdain of every artistic factor in culture. The fine arts originate in the play-instinct of man. They are bound to develop somewhat in directions of trivial amusement, of idle luxury, and even of positive folly. They are often most showy where the moral values of life and the higher energies of society are least regarded or most perverted. Consequently it has sometimes been assumed that the most petty aspects of all the arts are the most characteristic, and that their nobler developments are too exceptional to be counted. Art has not seldom been considered only a surface decoration of life, wholly incidental and accidental to its real substance. Music, of all the fine arts, has perhaps been the most subjected to this sort of depreciation.

. . . . . .

American musicians have for a long time been struggling for a universal recognition of singing as a necessary topic of regular instruction in the public schools, beginning, of course, in the cities and large towns. The claim is that this is only fair to the subject and to the pupils. The schools have begun to see that popular education means more than languages, mathematics, physical science and history. The moment they admit that literary and æsthetic culture is needed to make full-rounded men and women, and that some acquaintance with the processes and products of the fine arts, literature included, is needed to prepare their pupils to enter understandingly into the life of the world, they must admit music on some sort of parity with other arts. Most of the arguments for modeling, drawing, painting, yes, for essay-writing, might be urged also for singing. The gain in this direction has so far been principally in the lower grades, in the kindergarten, the primary school, and the grammar school. The high schools are less cordial. Some of the colleges as yet show almost an antipathy to music, except as a detached specialty. Several of them, it is true, especially those for women or for both sexes, have flourishing music schools affiliated with them or incorporated in their system, where much high-class technical work is done. But these advantages are chiefly confined to such pupils as have exceptional musical aptitude or, at least, an ambition to plume themselves with some showy, polite accomplishments. The connection of music with the general culture that is aimed at by the prescribed studies of the regular curriculum is avowedly slight. Finally, in institutions of a university grade there are a few instances of elaborate musical courses leading to academic degrees. These courses exert a wholesome influence in that they give a scholarly standing to musical study, and often splendidly equip those who follow them. But the number of students that enter them is relatively small, and naturally includes hardly any but those who intend to make music a profession. The distinction between such university courses and the best of the purely technical or specialistic music schools is slight.

This state of affairs has both a hopeful and a discouraging side. It must be admitted that there has been a great gain in recent years in the amount of our public instruction in music. There has been a steady and manifest improvement in the methods, the scope, and the purpose of such teaching. The *personnel* of the musical profession is far finer than it was even a generation ago. In consequence, through a variety of channels, of which public music teaching is certainly one of the most important, the significance and dignity of music as an object of effort have been decidedly advanced in popular estimation. Not only is it fashionable to become an instrumental or vocal performer, but the quiet diffusion of musical information through public instruction and through the increasing body of competent amateurs tends constantly to raise the average musical standard of our larger communities. Choral societies are slowly multiplying and plainly advancing in capacity. Concerts and recitals are becoming more frequent and better. Our church music is certainly improving at every point. The lift in the amount of popular enthusiasm about music is, on the whole, encouraging and promising.

But, on the other hand, one may venture to wonder whether this gain is all of the best sort, or, rather, whether it is coming to bear where it is most needed. How much consistent and determined effort is there to articulate musical study with *general* culture? If a boy or girl shows musical talent, the special cultivation of it is encouraged. If a fair number of people in a community can be induced to find enjoyment in such concerts as can be arranged, the taste for such enjoyment is fostered and fed in whatever ways are found to be pecuniarily feasible. But the training which results both of individuals and of the music-loving public tends to be over-special, too detached from other topics of public interest, uncorrelated or isolated. It is apt too often to make mere performers and mere critics of performance. Technique is the one goal of too many students, and brilliance of execution the one demand of too many listeners and patrons. While the stimulus is great for those of decided musical talent, those who show no special aptitude, and those who have no ambition of becoming technical experts, are overlooked and unprovided for. The keenness of audiences for a telling or *bravura* performance increases, but combined with it is too little discrimination as to the essential value of the works chosen for rendering. We get more and better technical musicians of a certain kind, but the average popular acquaintance with the immense literature of music is curiously limited, and the average sensitiveness to the inner meaning of musical works is curiously dull. In a word, something of the isolation of music which in the past came from its cultivation in an over-specialistic way is being perpetuated.

This is not to be taken as implying anything against the strictly specialistic training of those who are to give their lives to music as a profession. The purely technical opportunities now open to the musical aspirant are surely a source of pride and strength. Without them the art of music would presently begin to stagnate and then to deteriorate. Without them we should have no masters and leaders, no authorities, no freshness of creation, no sustained enthusiasm for the culminating triumphs of musical art. Nothing here is meant to detract from the importance of these vital processes whereby the professional organism of music is nourished and continually rejuvenated.

But how about the unprofessional side of the matter, the musical culture of the huge masses of people who will never be musicians in any technical sense, the creation of a popular sentiment about music that shall securely link it with the abiding interests of intellectual and spiritual life? It seems to me that musicians owe it to their art continually to revert to this question of the popularization of music, not simply because of a philanthropic interest in the musically ignorant and defective, but in justice to their own theory of the universal and glorious quality of music itself. Those who live in a musical atmosphere claim to derive therefrom something that makes them larger, higher, better men and women. They feel that this experience is due, not so much to an abnormal or entirely exceptional capacity in them that is non-existent in men generally, as to the enjoyment of special advantages and the development into full activity of powers that are at least potentially present in all men. In support of their view they often point rather proudly to the cosmopolitan character of modern music, with its growing independence of national and other boundaries, or solace themselves with some golden tribute to music's universal power from the great poets. Yet, if musicians cannot demonstrate in practice that music has a real, tangible value to all cultivated people as an integral part of their culture, and that therefore it should be a constituent of general education from bottom to top, having close inter-relations with other topics of such education, and supported by the same reasonable logic—if they cannot do this, then they are at least pursuing a phantom, if not sailing under false colors. Either music has the capacity and the right to be far more of a wide-working social force, or she is not worthy of the prodigious outlay of wealth and energy that is being lavished upon her.

If there be any cogency in these considerations, they bring us face to face with the necessity of suggesting something to be desired and sought. In yielding to this necessity, I offer a few thoughts along but one or two lines, though I fully realize that there is much more that may be said and perhaps needs to be said.

First of all let me urge that a larger emphasis should be thrown upon general education as a prerequisite for the popular exercise of musicianship. There are too many cases in which gifted enthusiasts push their way into prominence in the profession with so little breadth of information, so little discipline of all the mental faculties, so slight a sympathetic sense of the myriad interests and forces in our complex modern life, that they are really unable to see the problem here considered, much less to do anything effectively for its solution. Our age is one of specialism, it is true; but it is also an age of the close interaction and precise co-ordination of specialities. To pursue a specialty successfully is highly honorable, provided that the specialist knows where he is in the universe of thought. Greatness may consist largely in being a master in some one field; but greatness in helpless or ignorant isolation is at least half wasted, if not in danger of being half perverted. I cannot believe that in music, any more than in any other vocation, it is safe to expect the best success without genuine and enthusiastic comprehensiveness of contact with the actual life of humanity, such as is possible only for one whose education has been elaborate and well-rounded. This is a necessity for musicianship pure and simple; but it is incontestably a necessity for the delivery of music from its isolation as a popular power. Happily the signs of advance in this regard multiply on every hand.

Second, I would plead for the closer association of musical study with other forms of study. Whether or not it is practicable as yet to make music in its higher grades an actual constituent of the curricula of all schools, colleges, and universities may be doubted. But we may be eager to see every possible musical course put into close relation with other courses in all sorts of educational institutions. Musicians, indeed, may wish that every such introduction of music might be beyond criticism as to technical method. Yet, even where the work done is relatively feeble and fragmentary, the mere recognition of music as a topic of study in fellowship with other topics merits hearty support. Poorness of method may be left to rectify itself. It may be that the traditional methods of musical teachers need the stimulus of comparison with methods in other departments. The main thing is to secure a foothold for musical art in every accessible educational system, from the kindergarten to the university. It would surely be well, also, if our leading music schools were all in close proximity to institutions of recognized scholastic standing. Proximity provokes comparison, if not affiliation. The spirit of one school reacts helpfully on that of its neighbors. Interchange of students, of instructors and of books and other apparatus is facilitated. Education in the large sense means learning, dexterity in its use, power in independent mental action, and the development of a healthy personality. In any one institution the balance may be imperfectly struck. The close contact of different institutions tends to correct onesidedness in all. Music schools have sometimes ignored learning, strict scholarship, and real character-building. Other schools have too often ignored all æsthetic subjects, and have underrated the sensitiveness of feeling and the dexterity of action that is indispensable in art. Both classes may be benefited in ways too numerous to specify by being set side by side. In all these regards, too, the signs of advance are encouraging.

Third, I would especially plead for a closer study by musicians and by educators generally of the natural analogies between music and literature as branches of popular culture. I here refer not simply to the affinities that draw poetry and music together, though these finely illustrate my point. But I mean that in solving the problem of fully bringing music into its place in general education, the essential likeness of it to literature should be accepted and adopted as a principle of action. "Literature," as the term must be used by a professional educator, includes not only works but workings, both expressive and impressive. The great function of literature in the world, I assume, is the clear, adequate, and forcible intercommunication of personalities through the medium of language, and its importance as a field of education follows from the fact that no other form of intercommunication is so full, so infinitely varied, and so universally powerful. The point here urged is that, since the analogy between literature and music is far closer and more complete than is usually perceived, the educational treatment of the two should be deliberately similar. Upon this, one of the most pregnant of themes, there is space for but a few rapid and scattered suggestions.

Literature has for its vehicle speech. Music's vehicle is tone. The two combine in song. How close to each other are the processes of speaking and singing is best known to technical students of the two as fine arts. The experience of vocal teachers constantly reinforces the belief that the highest results in both directions depend on the frank recognition of their common ground in the use of the voice as an instrument of personal expression. A sound discipline of the literary sense, and of the musical sense as well, depends primarily on a thorough vocal training of every student of either. The schools are fairly ready to acknowledge the value of reading aloud as a basis for literary interpretation and for literary composition. Hand in hand with this ought to go a parallel use of singing as a basis for musical interpretation and musical composition. These propositions are not merely theoretical; they have been nobly demonstrated by the most progressive teachers. But the demonstrations have thus far been mostly confined to the lower grades of study. They need to be carried up into the higher grades also. One of the most famous of our teachers of English literature, Prof. Hiram Corson, has

recently said that the inward experience of the greatest master-
pieces of our literature is absolutely impossible without the
constant use by both teacher and pupil of actual vocal interpretation. His view is shared by an increasing number of his fellow-
instructors. It may be questioned whether in the musical field
we shall make the best progress until singing is restored to its
full place as the paramount and normative musical process for
every student.

But this is only one side of the subject. In literary study it
is clearly seen that breadth and accuracy of culture depend
chiefly, not on the mere minute preparation of single extracts
for elocutionary delivery, but on the intelligent analysis of and
the sympathetic familiarity with large numbers of works by
many masters, on many subjects, in many styles, and appealing
to many susceptibilities. "Reading," said Lord Bacon, "maketh
a full man"—meaning copious private reading for information
and scope. Is it not the same with music? Technique—literary
or musical—is a means, not an end. It is a necessary servant
of culture, but a sorry object of worship. May we not hope that
the time will come when all music teachers shall see that the
goal of their work is not the preparation of isolated pieces for
performance, but the cultivation in every student of the power
to know for himself at first hand many works, by all sorts of
composers, in every known form, even including hundreds that
never are and never can be prepared for perfect performance?
And the power to read music readily and copiously should be
made to lead to an insatiable desire to go on doing so till something of the whole range of musical literature is gone over. To
be a somewhat striking performer may co-exist with an altogether petty and paltry musicianship, just as many an elocutionist
and actor is only a literary tyro or poltroon.

The same principle applies to concert-hearing. No one would
be called a true lover of literature who merely busied himself
with hearing a series of declamations of a few well-known pieces,
simply applauding each succeeding conquest of their hackneyed
technical difficulties. Yet how many concert-goers pride themselves on a love for music when they are simply seeking the
excitement of witnessing successive acrobatic feats with the

fingers or the larynx. How many otherwise cultivated people have to be laboriously taught as if they were mere children to hear with reverence all the great musical works of the past, and to welcome with eagerness those of the present. Concert-going always involves the insidious danger that a lower impulse shall be mistaken for a higher, that the mere sensuous craving for a transient gratification shall be confounded with the real thirst for permanent musical culture. Happily, this danger is always being opposed by the better class of performers, to whom interpretation is as sacred and noble an art as composition, and in whose hands the creations of the past are being continually made new.

One more working out of this analogy between literature and music may be suggested. The ablest teachers of literature know that their highest mission is not to teach prose or poetry in and for themselves, as mere objective products, but to show how in these products humanity has expressed itself, how the author's personality is declared, how the author represents a period, a class, or a tendency of human development, and how in the utterance universal thoughts and sentiments are embodied and universal sensibilities touched. It is the proud boast of literature that to study it in any proper way is to study and to know *man* in the fullest sense. I cannot but believe that music and musical education will remain somewhat isolated and fruitless until a precisely analogous ambition becomes thoroughly operative there. Musicians may devote themselves to the mechanism of composition or performance, may range eagerly over the whole field of musical works and styles, may become even learned in formal analysis and technical criticism, and yet these achievements will be but small unless through all this their pupils are steadily gaining in a vital, hearty, spiritual sympathy with composers and performers as representative men, and through them with the essential life of mankind.

These analogies between music and literature might be much extended and profusely illustrated. But this need not be done here. It only remains to say that the responsibility for working out the problems here suggested seems to rest mainly with musicians themselves. The limitations and perversions of their art in popular estimation and handling are familiar to them. So far as these remove it from contact with human interests and efforts generally, or dissociate it from other artistic and literary fields to which it is strictly analogous, the resulting isolation demands closest study and most determined efforts at reform. While it is true that much is due to music and to musicians from the outside world which has not yet been cordially and universally granted, it is also true that justice from others cannot rightfully be expected so long as those who profess and call themselves musicians are not ready to render it themselves to their own magnificent art. If music deserves to become less isolated than she has been in common thought and especially in education, musicians must be foremost in believing it and in proclaiming and exemplifying their belief. Music will be to the world what musicians make it. It may for a time be something less; but it never can be more.

The hope of the matter, therefore, lies in the earnest efforts within the profession in various ways so fully and justly to set forth what music really is, and so logically and conscientiously to keep it in its due relations with its sister arts, and especially with literature, that the recognition which the earnest world is ever ready to give to whatever is true may more and more deliver music as an art, musicians as artists, and the glorious literature of tone-poems and tone-dramas which music has been for centuries producing and reproducing, from the sad and false isolation in which they have too often been placed in social life, in education, and in historic and philosophic criticism.

16. GRAND OPERA IN AMERICA

HEINRICH CONRIED

The first question asked by the average American opera-goer on the approach of a new season is, "What singers have been engaged this year?" After that he may express curiosity as to the works which the singers are likely to interpret. It would be absurd for the director of an institution like the Metropolitan Opera House to affect ignorance of the popular attitude towards lyric drama. In the interest of art, he may regret it. Or, if he be only a man of business, he may accept the facts dispassionately, as part of an existing order of things which must be recognized. Let it suffice for the moment that, rightly or wrongly, the American opera-goer is still more concerned about the singers than about the operas which are presented to him. And having admitted this much, with due philosophy, let us see in what particulars my second season at the Metropolitan Opera House will differ from my first.

A glance at the names of the chief artists in the Metropolitan company this year and last will enable one to perceive considerable changes. Circumstances of various kinds have prevented the re-engagement of several distinguished singers who were here last season. On the other hand, famous artists, hitherto strange to America, have been added to the company, together with several old favorites.

Last year, for reasons which need not be gone into, it was not possible to secure the co-operation of some artists who have since been added to the company. Nor, in a first and in a way experimental season, could one demand of me the smoothness, finish and general excellence which will, I trust, gradually become noticeable in performances at the Metropolitan Opera House. On assuming the direction of that theater, I at once perceived the necessity not only of rebuilding the stage, which was pitiably lacking in mechanical and electrical resources, but also of renovating the auditorium. When I remind the reader

Leslie's Monthly Magazine, 59 (January, 1905), 243–52.

that the work of reconstructing the stage was not completed till the twenty-first of November last year—*two days* before the opening of the season with "Rigoletto"—the difficulties which beset my path may be imagined. One of the worst difficulties was the fact that, under the system which obtained at the time when my immediate forerunner withdrew from the cares of management, the stage hands and technicians, including "property men" scene-shifters, electricians, carpenters and wardrobe men, were engaged only for the season. During the rest of the year they had to provide for themselves as best they could. One result of this system may, indeed, have been a diminution of expense. But another was a lamentable loss of general efficiency, which was evident in the Metropolitan productions. This season, the heads of the technical departments, and all the stage hands, have been engaged by the year. As a consequence the interest of the workmen in their duties has naturally quickened. I may add, too, that I have engaged a special staff of stage hands to work from midnight, after the performances, till morning. This, also, I found indispensable, as, owing to the smallness of the Metropolitan Opera House stage, as compared with the stages of the great lyric theaters of Europe, it was necessary to remove the scenery each night to neighboring storehouses to make way for other scenery. In Paris, Vienna, Munich, Dresden, Prague, Milan, Naples and other centers of musical art, each opera house is provided with a back-stage, almost and sometimes quite as large as the one seen by the public. On this back-stage the scenes used in the various productions can be built and prepared for each successive act, much to the benefit of the performances. Nothing of the kind is possible at the Metropolitan. The annual increase in the cost of the productions made here since the introduction of the reforms just mentioned is about fifteen thousand dollars.

The abuses of the old methods which have now been definitely reformed were often heartbreaking. Here is an example. Before the production of "Die Walküre," a year ago, with Mr. Fuchs and Mr. Lautenschlaeger I devoted two whole afternoons to special rehearsals of the calcium light men. Having at last taught them exactly what were their respective duties, as a measure of precaution I gave all of the men a written set of instructions, imploring them to see that they obeyed them strictly. To my amazement I then learned for the first time that the men whom I had so laboriously drilled were not operators, but mere helpers, and that, though they had rehearsed in the afternoon, they would be replaced by a new set of workmen at the actual performance. Is it strange if, when evening came, there were flaws and hitches in the lighting of "Die Walküre"? This season the public should have less cause to complain of imperfect lighting at all events. Probably, too, thanks to the superior skill and discipline of the Metropolitan stage hands, I shall be able to shorten the entr'actes.

Other improvements will, I hope, be apparent in the chorus, the "supers" and the *corps de ballet* of the theater. I have largely recruited the male "supers" from the ranks of educated applicants, including college men, and men who have had military training. On the Continent, it is customary for the directors of important opera houses to draw freely on the local garrisons for the "supers" they require. All they need to do is to notify the commanding officers, who at once place at their disposal ten, fifty or a hundred of their subordinates. I may be permitted also, to call attention to my efforts to abolish the old, stupid, traditions which made the Metropolitan chorus a laughing stock. For generations the ladies and gentlemen of the chorus had been accustomed, regardless of dramatic proprieties or plausibilities, to stand in certain places on the stage, to make certain conventional gestures, and to form certain groups. It was common for them, when they should have been welcoming someone arriving from the back of the stage, to address their invocation, and express their enthusiasm, not to the arrivals but—to the family circle. Little by little, these inconsistencies, and many other absurdities, will disappear. But I dare not promise that they will vanish suddenly or utterly in one season.

American opera-goers, I am convinced, have but a vague idea of the responsibilities, the labors and the difficulties of the director of the New York opera house. His fortunate brethren in the cities of the Old World have enormous advantages. They are not hurried in the task of preparing new productions. They have permanent companies made up of artists engaged at annual salaries, and required by their contracts to appear in any parts, whether they be large or small, for which they are fitted. They receive subsidies, which relieve them of the fears of financial failure. They are not expected to secure the services of sensationally fine singers. Their orchestras, like their singers, are engaged for an extended time and devote themselves exclusively to opera. Conditions here are very different. The shortness of the season forbids the director of the Metropolitan Opera House to engage his vocal artists, musicians, chorus, "supers" and ballet permanently, and therefore it is out of the question to give ideal performances. In many ways, no doubt, grand opera, as we know it here, is infinitely finer, more brilliant and more satisfying to our own public than anything to be found in Europe might be. But, except as to the singing, it is not ideal, in the same sense as grand opera in Vienna, under the direction of Mahler, may be called ideal. No European management would ever dream of spending the fortunes that are paid yearly in New York for the salaries of singers (to mention only one and the chief item in the grand opera budget). To illustrate the difference between the American and European systems, I may recall that, rather than pay Faure—the greatest of all French barytones—about three hundred dollars a performance, the then management of the Paris Opera House allowed that wonderful artist to retire from the stage. Everything in America, so far as opera is concerned, costs vastly more than it does abroad.

Then, again (and this brings me back to a point on which I have just touched), the director of the Metropolitan is hampered at every turn by being compelled to guarantee the chief singers in his company a stipulated number of appearances within stipulated times, and on stipulated terms which, to the non-initiate, might seem incredible. The difficulty is further complicated by the fact that certain artists are paid so much for each performance, not so much for the season. Imagine the ingenuity needed to so vary and select the repertory as to allow the talent of each singer to be fully utilized and in exactly the way called for by each contract. Madame A is to appear twice a week and to receive so and so many hundreds or thousands of dollars on each occasion. Mr. B is to sing so many times a month. Mlle. C is assured so and so many opportunities in a season. And, somehow or other, the exigencies of these artists have to be reconciled with the moral necessity of producing such and such operas, music-dramas and ballets during the brief space of about four months.

In the existing circumstances the repertory itself, to some extent, depends on the composition of the company and the agreements which the chief singers have signed with the management. Still more does it depend on conditions of time and space. Each week I am compelled to give at least six performances of grand opera. On Mondays, Wednesdays, Fridays and Saturday afternoons there are "subscription" performances; Thursdays are reserved for "Parsifal," and Saturday nights are devoted to what are called "performances at popular prices." On Sundays, too, there are the concerts. All these performances involve rehearsals, and I have but one stage at my disposal. Months were exceptionally devoted to preparing the production of "Parsifal." As a rule, however, one week is the utmost that can be spared for rehearsing a new work, whereas in Europe it is quite usual to give up a year to getting an important work ready. The marvel, perhaps, is—not that new works are so seldom seen there, but that they are seen so often. A single production like that of "Aida" demands the services of close upon four hundred persons, exclusive of the musicians in the orchestra and the stage hands. The "casting" of an opera is in itself no trifle. Enormous "cachets" (or "fees") cannot be paid in exchange for small services. It would, therefore, be folly to allot a minor part to a great singer, as Mahler can afford to do in Vienna, where the artists, as I have already explained, have annual salaries and appear in whatever parts may be allotted to them. Besides, even if the director of the Metropolitan were willing to squander money to attain a standard of ideal excellence, he would have to contend with personal vanity, artistic jealousy and abnormal sensitiveness. Mme. A, whose remuneration for one night would keep many a large family for a whole year, would decline to sing any but the most

conspicuous feminine rôle. Mr. B would be equally refractory
if his dignity were slighted by the offer of anything less than
the leading barytone part. Mr. C, the tenor, would probably
risk losing his whole season's emoluments rather than interpret
anything but the hero of the opera in which he was to appear.
Even the bassos (who are usually more amiable and easy to
live with than the sopranos and tenors, or some barytones)
would have objections to being cast for parts less portentous
than those of the kings, landgraves and high-priests of grand
opera. The preferences, prejudices and peculiarities of five or
six prima-donnas, as many tenors and about the same number
of barytones and bassos, have to be considered throughout the
season at the Metropolitan, or—as things stand—grand opera,
on the scale to which Americans have grown used, could not
be given. Abroad, directors are less fettered and it is much
easier to deal with artists. Another stumbling-block that renders
it hard to enlarge the repertory is the unwillingness of the
"stars" to learn new parts, which they may never be able to
sing outside of America. So long as these "stars" are conspicuous in the operatic firmament, so long is the repertory at the
Metropolitan likely to be limited. Despite drawbacks, I still hope
to present about forty operas and two ballets this season,
including half a dozen semi-novelties and elaborate revivals.
"Gioconda," "Lucrezia Borgia" and "La Favorita," which are
among the revivals, will be virtually new to a majority of our
opera-goers. "Der Fliegende Holländer," though to most familiar, has been neglected for some years. And it is safe to say
that, in the new setting which I have had made for it in Vienna,
"Die Meistersinger" will, at least pictorially, seem a revelation.

Those Wagner-lovers, who last season occasionally re-
proached me for reviving the old Italian operas, will doubtless
find fault with me again this year, notwithstanding my production of "Parsifal," for resuscitating "Lucrezia Borgia" and "La
Favorita." I shall not attempt an apology for being more liberal
in my ideas with regard to opera than my hostile critics. There
is room for all good music at the Metropolitan; for "Fidelio"
and for "Un Ballo in Maschera;" for "Carmen" and for "Tris-
tan;" for "Pagliacci" and for "Parsifal."

So much, then, for the past and present of grand opera at the Metropolitan. As to its future, it lies with the public rather than with the director to decide whether it shall flourish, more or less, on the lines with which we are familiar, or whether it shall be modified by the addition of the vernacular to the other languages in which it is now interpreted. Permanent grand opera, as it is understood in Vienna, Paris or Berlin, we can hardly hope to see established here. But by degrees something may be accomplished toward the interpretation of grand opera by English-speaking and English-singing artists of international importance in the idiom of our own land. This would, of course, seem the ideal. Unhappily, the obstacles in the way of its realization are serious and, in the near future, perhaps insuperable. Not because there is not material enough awaiting development in America—I have convinced myself that, so far at all events as female voices are concerned, there is more and finer material to draw on in this country than even in Italy—but because opportunities are lacking for that steady, patient and gradual training of opera singers which can be had in Europe. I have been astonished to find that, of the many hundreds of young singers who have applied for admission to the School of Opera which I have founded at the Metropolitan, and of those who have come to me for engagements in the chorus, almost all could read music at sight easily, while most were able, if desired, to sit down at the piano and play their own accompaniments. Musical culture of this kind among operatic aspirants is rare, even in Germany.

Where, however, is our budding operatic talent to be trained? Where is it to be developed? Where is it to have opportunities of maturing and of fitting itself for eventually shining at the Metropolitan?

In France and Germany, which have opera houses in all the great cities and in many a small center, similar problems are solved easily. Here, with the exception of one French company in New Orleans and one English company without a home, there had hitherto been no operatic organizations in which beginners gradually cultivate their voices and acquire dramatic art till they were ready to brave criticism in the metropolis.

Within a measurably short time, maybe, I shall venture on some special performances—at very "popular" prices—with the pupils of my School of Opera. I am not particularly optimistic, though, as to the practical results that will come of the experiment, so far as American engagements are concerned. Possibly, the success of my School of Opera pupils will lead to their securing engagements abroad. I have discussed the subject lately with various European directors, and many of them seem willing to co-operate with me in my plan for the encouragement and assistance of the young American opera singers.

As far as the singers of established reputation are concerned, the company at the Metropolitan Opera House challenges comparison with any that has been known here, while it is enormously superior to the rival organizations of Europe. . . .

VI

The Theater

Any town worth its slogans boasted an "opera house," or all-purpose theater that symbolized connections with the larger world. Little grand opera appeared on such stages, though touring companies regularly offered operettas and truncated versions of larger works. The "opera house" usually hosted plays and variety, and theatergoing was doubtless the most widespread evidence of public interest in culture. Until movies and television displaced it, live drama was important at most levels of American life.

This was especially evident in the late 19th century. Efficient railroad service, with connections to every sizable town, allowed impresarios to expand tours. Graphic advertisements heightened the expectations of potential audiences. Public relations techniques created and sustained a glamorous star system. And technology improved lights, costumes, sets, and audience comforts.

A great variety of vehicles fell under the rubric "theater," and more people doubtless applauded melodrama than drama. Shakespeare remained the staple of the American stage. Farce, variety, adventure, and a few durable spectacles like "Ben Hur" and "The Count of Monte Cristo" were common items in rural fare. But by the 1890s a new realistic treatment and subject matter had filtered into all levels of theater production. Sharp social comment united the themes of many seemingly innocuous plays. The stage did not become the preserve of a wealthy or closed class, and revealed the impact of new demands and problems in an urban-industrial society. For expertise and sophistication, the stage of 1900 was far removed from that of preceding generations.

New York and the major cities remained the founts of legitimate theater. Their producers and audiences were more innovative, tolerant and wealthy than those in smaller cities. They supported excellent productions of the exciting new realistic works of Ibsen and Shaw, among others. Foreign plays, like foreign paintings, were new connections to the world, expanding the theater's coverage and vitality.

The theater revealed the stresses and confusions of public tastes following a sudden input of ideas. Because of its immediacy, drama was always a target of moralistic reformers. Growing realism, and concern for broad social questions made it a subject of sharp debate as old ideals and tastes were challenged.

Whatever the controversies, Americans went to the theater in unprecedented numbers. Some went for escape, some for uplift. Others went to sample new things in the art form. Whatever their motive, they gained a new view of a changing world.

17.   THE AMERICAN DRAMA REVISITED

WILLIAM ARCHER

. . . First, a few words as to material conditions. New York
is, on the whole, I take it, a better field than London for theatrical enterprise. The habit of theater-going is more widely diffused.
The main body of the theatrical public lives nearer to the region
of the theaters, or, at any rate—thanks to the "Elevated," the
electric cars and the Subway—can reach it more expeditiously
and cheaper. The dearest seats are somewhat cheaper than in
London, the cheapest seats somewhat dearer—which is probably, on the whole, an advantage. But the greatest advantage of
all lies in the fact that the evening-dress habit is by no means
so tyrannical and deterrent in New York as in London. The
busy New Yorker does not feel bound to go home and dress
before going to the play. If he has time to dress, good and well;
if not—no matter. Nor do his womankind hold it necessary to
dress (and undress) themselves as tho for a ball before they
enjoy an evening's amusement at the theater. From the business
point of view the beneficial effect of this common-sense treatment of the dress question is incalculable. How many thousands
of people in London are driven to the music halls simply because
they have not time or energy to dress for the theater! Yet I know
of only one London manager—Mr. George Alexander—who
has declared himself hostile to the evening-dress superstition.

That impermanence of American buildings which so dis-
tresses Mr. Henry James is clearly illustrated in the case of the
New York theaters. Of those which I visited in 1899 few have
survived the intervening eight years. Most of them have either
vanished entirely or sunk into variety shows; while the constant
uptown movement has brought into being a whole cluster of
new theaters about the intersection of Broadway and Forty-
second street. Eight years ago the theatrical region was fairly
well lighted of an evening; but now the blaze of electricity which

The Independent, 62 (June 27, 1907), 1519–25.

has earned for these streets the title of "The Great White Way," is, I believe, unparalleled in any other city.

But in one respect New York is distinctly, and rather alarmingly, behind London. We, too, in the past ten years, have built many theaters, and we have built them with much greater regard to safety than is manifested in New York. I believe I am right in saying that our building regulations require that at least half of the peripheral line of a theater shall stand free from contact with any other building—which practically means that a theater cannot be built except on a corner site. As a matter of fact, many of our recent theaters stand free on three sides, if not on all four. Not so in New York. Here theaters are jammed together or sandwiched between other buildings, with what strikes me as extraordinary recklessness. Many of them have an absurdly narrow frontage, so that in order to reach the street the audience from all parts of the house have to converge in one wholly inadequate corridor or vestibule. This dangerous condition of things may in some cases be mitigated by iron emergency staircases outside the building; but for my part I should have little confidence in these appliances in case of a panic. The authorities seem to put pathetic trust in the system of numbering every doorway in the auditorium, "Exit 1," "Exit 2," and so forth up to "Exit 10" or even "Exit 20," and printing on each program a plan of the theater with these exits marked. But fancy an audience studying a little ill-printed plan with the smoke of a conflagration beginning to roll thru the house! Besides, a doorway is not in any valid sense an "exit" unless there be a corresponding opening, easily reached, in the outer wall of the building. A dozen "exits," all debouching ultimately into one narrow passage, are equivalent to just the width of that passage and no more. I sincerely trust that the measures taken to prevent an outbreak of fire are better than those for securing the safety of the audience should a conflagration, or a groundless panic, occur.

The immunity of America from the evening-dress superstition is much more significant than it might appear at first sight. The swallow-tail dominates the London stage no less than the London auditorium. To the British drama the white choker is a choker indeed. The dramatist cannot escape from the draw-ing-room, the boudoir and the conservatory. When he needs a breath of fresh air, he must be content to take it at a garden party. Sometimes, indeed, he may visit a country inn, but it must be in the society of an eloping Countess. On rare occa-sions he may indulge in an excursion to a Scotch moor in order to study its traditional fauna—to wit, dukes, millionaires and flunkies with luncheon baskets. Outside Great Britain only two places exist for him—Paris and Monte Carlo. He is fettered, in a word, to the West End of London. Even when he seems to wander from it, he but drags a lengthening chain. He may go wherever the West End of London goes; but elsewhere—at his peril! At the outset of his career, Mr. Pinero attempted, as he said, "to get the scent of hay across the footlights"; but this he soon abandoned.

The American dramatist suffers from no such petty restric-tion. The whole wide field of American life is open to him, and he is rapidly learning to make good use of his freedom. As people come to the theater in their workaday clothes, so they are willing to interest themselves in all aspects of the workaday world. There is probably a certain class—perhaps a large class —which still actively prefers the drama of dress coats and Paris gowns, such as our English playwrights turn out. In 1899 the manager of a huge stock company theater in Boston, which gave two performances a day and changed its bill every week, told me that his audiences, among whom women largely pre-ponderated, were devoted admirers of the "shirt front play." No doubt this frame of mind still obtains to a certain extent. It is only too natural that people—and especially women— whose own lives are gray, laborious and sordid, should love to dwell in an imaginary world of light and luxury, purple and fine linen. That is the reason, I take it, why many of our English plays are still in request at cheap stock-company theaters, when their term of life in London or at the Broadway theaters is long over. But the American public, as a whole, has no exclu-sive affection for dukes and millionaires. It has a keen apprecia-tion of character-study in all walks of life, of domestic senti-ment, and of that "ethical" criticism which is at present so much in the air. The astonishing growth of politico-social interest and intelligence which is manifested in the popular 10-cent magazines, finds its reflex, faint, indeed, but unmistakable, in the theater. On the whole, then, I find the conditions of theatrical life much more free and healthy in America than in England. In point of individual endowment, our English playwrights have still the advantage. America has as yet no such master craftsman as Mr. Pinero, no such delicate dramatic humorist as Mr. Barrie, no such playwright-sophist as Mr. Bernard Shaw. But were I a young dramatist, ambitious of developing my genius freely, I would shake the dust of Britain from my feet, plunge into American life, and try to depict it for the American people. There are wider opportunities in New York than in London.

The American drama of today may be roughly classified under four heads. In the first place, we have plays of society, of New York and Newport, of gambling and divorce, very much like the drawing-room dramas of the English stage. Then we have what may be rather too pompously entitled sociological plays—plays, I mean, which are more or less directly concerned with economic and political problems. The third class consists of domestic dramas, depicting middle-class life in town or country—"shirt sleeves" plays they have been not inaptly called. In the fourth class we may place such pieces as depend largely, and in some cases exclusively, upon external picturesqueness. They are dramas, for the most part, of frontier life in one or another of its phases.

Of the American social plays, one may say, in general terms, that they are written with somewhat less technical ability, and somewhat more intimate knowledge of the facts, than our English plays of the same type. The American playwrights who deal in this style of drama are much more genuinely at home in fashionable New York than are the British playwrights in fashionable London. They do not observe and report from an outside point of view, but are native and to the manner born.

. . . . .

Lower middle-class life is regarded on the English stage as exclusively a subject for farce or melodrama. The domestic drama of the mid-Victorian period has entirely died out. It was poor stuff, sometimes founded on French originals, always, or almost always, inspired by conventional, Dickensish sentiment. But why, when the "renascence" came in the late eighties, should domestic drama, instead of putting on new life, have been suffered to pine away and die? Why should a whole wide and deep stratum of English life have ceased to find any serious interpretation on the stage? Mainly, I think, because the long-run system caused the managers to vie with each other in luxurious mounting; so that richly upholstered scenes, peopled by ladies in gorgeous frocks and frills, came to be regarded as essential to success. The managers' insistence on an upper-class environment led playwrights always to look upward in the social scale; and they soon had no eyes for the life of their own class or of that immediately below them. This has been a double-barrelled misfortune for the English drama. Upper-class life has been portrayed with insufficient knowledge, while middle-class life, and especially lower middle-class life, has not been portrayed at all.

The American stage, very naturally, has always been more democratic. It has never lost touch of rural life, of frontier life, of the low life of the cities. Even in the days of greatest depression, while imported drama from France and England was mainly in the ascendant, there was always an active production of domestic dramas, as a rule very unsophisticated in form, but with touches of genuine observation, and affording an opportunity for excellent character acting. . . .

In this survey, I have hastily reviewed a number of American plays which happened to come within my ken during a three weeks' stay in New York. But the mere enumeration of this little group of plays conveys but a faint idea of the extent to which, within the past ten years or so, the American stage has become self-supporting. The pieces mentioned have all been acted at leading theaters, by actors of prominence. They all hover on the confines of literature, and one or two of them come well within the boundary-line. But apart from these more or less conspicuous plays, there is a luxuriant undergrowth of native production, in the shape of farces, melodramas, musical extravaganzas, folk-plays of a more or less unsophisticated order, variety "sketches," adaptations of novels (for instance, of the famous "Jungle"), and romantic plays. . . .

But while America is more and more determined to write her own plays, and less and less inclined to rely on England or France for the staple of her dramatic fare, she is still much more hospitable than England to all sorts of exotic effort in the field of drama. This fact is partly due, no doubt, to the great intermixture of races and nationalities in the American public; but I think it may also be traced to the active study of modern dramatic literature at the leading universities, both for young men and young women. This study begets, or helps to beget, a numerous public which is interested, not merely in the drama of commerce, but in almost every manifestation of intellectual activity in dramatic form.

To give a few examples: Maeterlinck's "Monna Vanna" has been played with marked success by Madame Kalisch; both Tolstoy's "Powers of Darkness" and Ostrovsky's famous play, "The Storm," have been acted with considerable acceptance by professional players; Hauptman's "Sunken Bell," and Sudermann's "Johannes," have for years held a prominent place in the repertory of Mr. Sothern and Miss Marlowe; Miss Nance O'Neill has found Sudermann's "Johannisfeuer" an attractive production; Mr. Richard Mansfield has added to his current repertory Moliere's "Misanthrope" and Schiller's "Don Carlos." In short, many plays which in England are either not acted at all, or presented only to special audiences of pronounced literary tastes, are in America received with more or less appreciation by the general public.

This American receptivity is, however, most clearly apparent in the ready acceptance accorded to several of the plays of both Henrik Ibsen and Bernard Shaw. On the very night of my arrival in New York, "Mrs. Warren's Profession" was given for the last time at the Manhattan Theater, after a run of about a month. I saw this last performance, and found it attended by a very fair audience, which received the play, on the whole, quite intelligently. Once or twice they laughed in the wrong place; but really an audience is to be excused which does not

quite know what to make of such a play as "Mrs. Warren."
Mr. Shaw himself is so apt to laugh in the wrong place that he
cannot blame his public for doing so now and then. Simply as
a matter of taste, then, I am not very desirous of seeing these
plays offered to the miscellaneous audiences of provincial cities,
whether American or English. But the fact that it is for a
moment possible in America—that it should ever enter anybody's head to send them "on the road"—proves that the
American public has a many-sided receptivity unknown in
England.

A week or two later I came across Mr. Shaw's "Man and
Superman," at Nixon's Theater, Pittsburgh—execrably acted
(save by Mr. Robert Loraine), but received with evident
pleasure by a good audience. Imagine "Man and Superman"
in Middlesborough or Hanley!

But the acceptance of Ibsen in America is, after all, the final
proof of the point I am making—namely that the American
public shows a much livelier curiosity in things theatrical than
the English. I say "curiosity," because to say "intelligence"
would, perhaps, be to beg a question. To be quite frank, one
is not greatly struck by the intelligence with which one commonly hears Ibsen discussed. But the frequency with which he
is acted, and the persistency with which he is discussed, show
that, if they do not quite understand him, the American public
are at any rate eager to get at the heart of his mystery. Their
mistake lies, indeed, in their determination to see mysteries and
enigmas where none exist, and where plain common-sense,
helped out with a little imagination, affords all necessary
guidance.

Within a month or so of my arrival in New York, six of
Ibsen's plays were performed in that city. . . .

18. THE STAGE AS A MORAL INSTITUTION

HENRY DAVIES

The present state of dramatic art in this country hardly war-
rants optimism. Our trouble is not an inadequate knowledge of
the splendid achievements of the past. Nor does it seem to be a
lack of insight into the sources of enjoyment afforded by the
present. It lies rather in our lack of a clear conception of the
relation of art to morals, a fact which naturally cuts us off from
the best in the past, and lowers the standard of the stage as we
now know it.

It may be assumed, in this critical review, that dramatic art
depends for its power and permanence, *as art,* upon its ability
to stir our emotions and to instruct our minds through speech
and action, so that we are led to form sound judgments about
life. The drama that does not both please and instruct, that
does not compel a judgment of approval or disapproval at the
same time that it kindles our senses with the pleasing mask of
acting, is, I take it, defective drama. Not that certain forms of
acting—vaudeville, for example—may not make pleasure more
obviously the object than instruction. This is freely admitted.
But even these more imitative forms of dramatic art cannot be
artistic, and simply amuse us, without injuring the influence of
the stage. It is not only false as art, but it is bad morals,—and
bad art is always bad morals,—for all art, and therefore dramatic art, must hold up the mirror of truth to life and make us
pleased with the portrayal.

We are, æsthetically, a very crude nation. Our taste is still
decidedly imitative and sensual, fond of show—spectacular. It
is also true that we are daringly experimental, and use every
means to familiarize ourselves with the materials and possibilities of art. We certainly have a great future especially in dramatic and musical art. But at present the imitative and the
sensual have the boards. The bulk of plays recently produced
on American soil are light, realistic, mirthful, representing no

special philosophy of life; they are written to charm and amuse, not to impress us morally. Even the dramatization of successful novels, which has recently usurped the place of independent creation in dramatic literature, has only operated to confirm this tendency. The practice is leading to the confusion of literary forms. For the novelist today must consider the chances he has of having his work reset for stage purposes, and this tends to turn the novelist into a play-writer. On the other hand, the play-writer tends to become the mere adapter of other men's creations, and so the freedom of creation is curtailed. In either case the stage suffers in its *morale*. The effect of these things on the taste of the theatre-going public is not altogether beneficial. A play like "The Little Minister," for example, considered in itself, can have only good influences on an audience; but, after all, is it *art*? Is the dramatized novel creative stage work or *only* adaptation? For moral effect a novel may be staged; but for the highest dramatic effect the dramatized novel is never anything more than a temporary and partial success. Such plays fail of permanence—and will continue to fail—because the artist creates at second hand. A more serious fault lies in the fact that when the novel becomes a play it steps out of its own legitimate field of the imagination and ceases to be art, in order to become a sensuous reality. Only a nation that reads practically nothing but novels will accept its plays thus at second hand. This is a sign of our crudity in matters of art. It is more than doubtful if the Russians or Germans would value a play like Hall Caine's "The Christian," or even "Quo Vadis?" as staged among us.

The present condition of dramatic art, as represented by the stage, shows that what is lacking is a serious motive to create true works of art, a purpose to instruct as well as amuse. It shows as well that a serious public is lacking. It is these persons that are involved in the task of raising the stage to its position as a moral institution. Let us see how.

The first condition of improvement is, of course, the production of a genuine dramatic literature, built upon the best models, reflecting the ideal of beauty, and yet representing life; a literature that shall not be ashamed of comparison with the classics, and at the same time be true to its own psychological and sociological climate; a literature that is sufficient as art and at the same time concrete enough for practical purposes; a literature that by its very spirit and diction tends to dignify the actor in his own sight and raise the taste of the public that witnesses its interpretation. That such a literature is lacking is to be accounted for, primarily, by the fact that the motive to its creation is lacking. The practical play-writer, indeed, doubts if such a literature can be produced in our time. He argues that a play should not aim at literary perfection, nor seek to convey moral impressions. It should simply portray life as it is and leave the judgment of the observer to condemn or approve its morals. The controversy over "Sapho" showed this. There are, as the play-writer knows, limits to this view which have been defined in our law books and beyond which he dare not step without punishment. And I take exception with him on still deeper ground. The error of realism, from which our drama is suffering, consists in omitting from its view the higher nature of man. Now it is safe to say, I think, that no artist can create a work of enduring merit by limiting himself to this "higher" nature, or by studying *only* moral effect. The contention of realism is true so far as it goes: the material of art is life, life as we know it in its length, breadth, depth, and height; but life, the realist often fails to see, can be interpreted only from its highest levels. As soon as we see this, the vacuity of realism becomes so obvious that the ponderous claim about "life as it really is" becomes nothing but an illusion. The prick of sensation in art, as Professor James says, is the intrusion of the personal, and the essence of personality is moral struggle. If, therefore, the play-writer would create a dramatic literature that truly interprets life, he must puncture the impersonal realism so much affected in his practice and depict life as a conflict of character, or moral idealism.

But, the play-writer argues, shifting his base, dramatic art must often represent life without reference to the moral ideal, because the life of average humanity often lacks it and because "the public" resents its intrusion. It is such contentions as these that try the moral fibre of play-writers; and it is not surprising perhaps, considering poor human nature, that they mostly yield their assent. The idea seems to be that the stage is to mirror actuality without reference to a final cause or moral motive. Now, whatever may be the verdict of "the public," such representations cannot be considered good art; for bad morals is always bad art; nor would such plays be judged good by any properly qualified audience. In other words, the play-writer is bound to consider, not only the morals of his own creations, but also the effect such creations are likely to have on the morals of the public. This is a point in criticism too little reflected upon by play-writers and actors alike. All the fine spiritual subtlety of the drama is involved in it. I am not going beyond my book when I say that the great bulk of modern plays leaves the audience without any bracing sense of the meaning and value of life, but rather with a feeling of surfeit, as though the digestion had been over-taxed. How different the clear air of a Shakespearian comedy! How spontaneous, free, lifelike it all is! What a fine sense of proportion and finality is displayed! The contention of the modern play-writer that the average morality of the public does not permit the enjoyment of moral and elevating drama; that his business is to portray life as it is, is only the error of realism over again. The contention, at bottom (and here I return to my original point), involves the moral responsibility of the play-writer. Is it the duty of the dramatist to create permanent literature if he can? or is realism the true point of view? For my own part, as a critic, I do not hesitate to oppose the latter claim. As regards the former, the situation is plainly this: the noblest dramatic art bases itself on the higher motives. Given these motives, dramatic artists will naturally interpret life in terms of idealism; they will capture our senses only to reach our minds, and thence penetrate to the sanctuary of the soul. The plays produced under these conditions could not fail to elevate the stage. That the main drift of dramatic art is still sensual, pandering to the realistic idol, is due, in large measure, to the realistic atmosphere of the modern play.

Next to the creation of a dramatic literature free from the taint of servitude to realism, I think the largest responsibility for the reform of the theatre rests with the actor. Personal experience leads me to believe that, in many important respects, the actor is as great a factor as the play-writer; for he has his freedom to reject a play that is not thoroughly artistic. But the fact that actors study what the public wants shows that they, too, have made the fatal compromise which tends to lower the influence of the stage as a moral institution. And for the most part he finds that realism suits the spirit of the age, and realism, therefore, he will give his audiences. The consequence is, acting tends to become affected, strained, and unnatural—in a word, impersonal. Compare with this the acting of Booth or Barrett, which was thoroughly imbued with their own personality; it was sincere, earnest, even noble. We meet here, on the ground of the actor, the same problem that we met on the ground of the play-writer,—the problem of realism and idealism. It is one of the nicest questions in dramatic æsthetics whether actors should hide their personalities in the part played, or whether their own ideals should penetrate it. Differently stated: Should the actor be inwardly indifferent to his rôle, yet concerned to produce the right effect on the audience; or should he support his rôle with his own emotions, presuming they are the emotions appropriate to the part played? This question has been ably discussed by one of the best of modern critics, Mr. William Archer, in his little work entitled "Masks and Faces." The reply, in general terms, seems to be as follows: those actors produce the most artistic influence who are most successful in assuming, through sympathy, a perfect moral identity with the part they play, and think, *after this relation has been established,* of how to transmit their ideals to the audience; technique is second only to interpretation. The true actor thinks first of his own ideals of life and character; it is his task "to create the part,"—a work in which he may often go beyond anything dreamed of by the play-writer. Now this is a great undertaking, and the way it is done is the sure index to the conscientious work of the actor; for he has not only to make others realize the interior character of his impersonation, but he has also to conceive and carry the organism of the play and the preconceived dramatic goal of the composition in his mind as well. He has to do this without devitalizing either side—a task which requires not only a well-trained æsthetic intelligence, but moral insight of the highest kind as well. Now on the presupposition of realism the actor need not trouble himself about these complex questions. All he has to do is to hold up life as it is, to sink his own feelings; his part is "a mask," not literally "a face." I have already pointed out the error of this philosophy—its superficiality; and to it we may trace the absence of great actors on the stage to-day. True actors have invariably been idealists, *i.e.,* they have been artists as well as actors. Such do always impart an element of idealism, a dignity and moral value to any part they interpret, because they bring to it not only good training, sound technique, but also sincere purpose, large interpretative imagination, and a feeling for the fitness of things on the stage.

The educative influence of the stage is so great that the loss of the ideal side of the actor's art is missed more quickly there than anywhere. Actors must, therefore, lay this lesson to heart, that if they would elevate the taste of the people, if they would change the mode of judging of life, it must be by the influence of a nobly played part. The actor's "mask" should actually be a "face," in which the observer, his senses kindled and captured, sees the play of conflicting moral standards, and, by what he sees, is pleased and instructed—led, in a word, to form a healthy and sound judgment of art and life.

But there is another and final condition of reform—the education of public taste. The responsibility for the degenerate tendencies of the drama does not rest wholly on the play-writer and actor. The people, the great public—whose infallibility is not so unquestionable as certain French critics would have us believe—quite as often fail to appreciate the better kind of play through lack of dramatic education, and overwork. The latter cause—the fact that people are too tired in these days for serious drama—naturally creates the demand for amusement rather than instruction; though I think this demand is greatly exaggerated. We still remain, however, pathetically blind to the glories of Shakespeare, and conventional and unintelligent in regard to grand opera. Whether this state of things continues depends somewhat upon the question whether the strenuous commercialism of modern life continues, and whether we shall settle down to new and more worthy ideals of social evolution after the present acute phase of progress shall have been passed. Whilst it lasts the public is unfitted, by its habits of life, to enter into the higher and nobler elements of the drama; amusement is the chief need of our times and natures.

My hopes and fears for dramatic art centre round the task of creating right tastes among the people. This is a large work, which some have already prejudged to be impossible of consummation, but without proper investigation. The stage will never lose its hold on the public. The only question is where to begin to make it the vehicle of the best influences. Now I think three things are obvious here. In the first place, much can be expected from the gradual introduction of art studies into our schools, colleges, and universities. The drama has not yet come in for its share of attention, but it surely will, as soon as our teachers are as wise as Froebel and Pestalozzi. Surely the time is not far distant when a man's education will include so much knowledge of art as will enable him to judge what is good drama, or to come to it able to feel highly, and judge its nobler qualities. An intelligent recognition of the equality of æsthetic with ethic and logic as a "culture-interest" is a step which is as inevitable as the progress of human thought, and I cannot see why this step should not be taken soon. What is needed is money to endow "chairs" in our universities devoted to the study and teaching of matters relating to the culture of the feelings. Here is, indeed, a new and attractive field for our millionaires. Pious founders in the past gave their money to endow chairs of logic, metaphysics, and theology. There are, perhaps, enough of these, at least for the present. But art is hardly even recognized in the modern university, and we wonder at the low state of the public taste!

Another step which would greatly aid the recovery of the moral functions of the stage is the cultivation of closer relations with other institutions which have direct bearing on the education of public taste. The weakness of the stage is due largely to its isolation; it often lacks the interest which comes from close contact with the life of the people; modest and sensible people often think of it as a sort of hothouse where nothing but exotics are raised. How true this judgment is is seen from the biographies of actors, which, for the most part, are melancholy reading, because their lives are so one-sided. Let the stage and the dramatic profession keep close to the life of men. Let them not despise any institution which shapes in any way, however small, the tastes of the public. The stage can learn something for its own good from the church, the political meeting, the struggle of the democracy for supremacy, and from the world-movements which stir the heart of humanity in these days.

Finally, we should form the practice of attending only the best dramatic performances and exert our influence against any and all forms of the degradation of the stage. If people of culture and intelligence were more positive in approving good plays, bad ones would be more easily crowded out. The moral elevation of the stage depends upon the encouragement afforded to the *best* in dramatic creation and acting, and if those best able to judge are not outspoken in approval where there is merit, how shall the public know what lead to follow?

These are but the merest hints in this great problem, but I think that if they were followed the stage would gradually feel a new spirit taking possession of it, the outward and visible token of which would be, first, an independent dramatic literature bearing the marks not only of patient labor but of inspiration, and, second, a new type of acting completely worthy of the best traditions of the profession. At present, it is to be feared, other influences prevail, though the outcome can hardly be in doubt, for art can never die. It springs, phoenix-like, out of the dead forms of unproductive periods, and, with newer inventions of beauty, resumes its pristine influence over men. So surely will it be with the modern stage when its moral mission is fully appreciated by play-writer, actor, and public.

BOOK MANUFACTURE

Victorian Culture in America, 1865–1914 was typeset, printed and bound at NAPCO Graphic Arts, Inc., New Berlin, Wisconsin. The cover design was by Evelyn Hansen, interior design by the F. E. Peacock Publishers, Inc., art department. The type is Times Roman.